MySQL®

PHRASEBOOK

ESSENTIAL CODE AND COMMANDS

Zak
Chris Newman

**DEVELOPER'S
LIBRARY**

Sams Publishing, 800 East 96th Street, Indianapolis, Indiana 46240 USA

MySQL® Phrasebook

Copyright © 2006 by Sams Publishing

International Standard Book Number: 0-672-32839-9

Library of Congress Catalog Card Number: 2005926873

Printed in the United States of America

First Printing: March 2006

09   08   07   06   4   3   2   1

Trademarks

Warning and Disclaimer

Bulk Purchases/Corporate Sales

Sams Publishing offers excellent discounts on this book when ordered in quantity for bulk purchases or special sales. For more information, please contact

U.S. Corporate and Government Sales
1-800-382-3419
corpsales@pearsontechgroup.com

For sales outside of the U.S., please contact

International Sales
international@pearsoned.com

Acquisitions Editor Shelley Johnston	**Production Editor** Heather Wilkins	**Publishing Coordinator** Vanessa Evans
Development Editor Damon Jordan	**Indexer** Erika Millen	**Designer** Gary Adair
Managing Editor Charlotte Clapp	**Proofreader** Dan Knott	
Project Editor George Nedeff	**Technical Editor** Tim Boronczyk	

Table of Contents

Contents

Contents

Appendix

About the Authors

Zak Greant is a free software and open source jack-of-all-trades. He works at eZ systems as the managing director of North American operations. Additionally, he is a Mozilla Foundation staff member and volunteers with the Free Software Foundation.

Chris Newman is a consultant programmer specializing in database development with an Internet twist. He has extensive commercial experience with using PHP to integrate various database systems and has produced a wide range of applications for an international client base. He runs Lightwood Consultancy Ltd, the company he founded in 1999 to further his interest in online database development. Newman is the author of *SQLite*, *Sams Teach Yourself PHP in 10 Minutes*, and *Sams Teach Yourself MySQL in 10 Minutes*.

Dedication

Zak would like to dedicate this book to
Deb and Tony.

Acknowledgments

As is the case with many books (even small ones), it takes a small village to successfully publish a book. While everyone who worked on the *MySQL Phrasebook* deserves thanks, particular recognition should be given to Shelley Johnston—this book would not exist without her determination and persistence. As they say, Shelley is crazy good.

Zak would also like to thank Chris, who saved the day; Jen, who did her best; Trudy, who offered sage advice; Damon, who was patient; Mandy, who was very, very patient; Mark, who was likely exceedingly patient; and the very nice security guard at Torp airport who set up a little space for me to pull an all-nighter trying to hit a chapter deadline.

We Want to Hear from You!

As the reader of this book, *you* are our most important critic and commentator. We value your opinion and want to know what we're doing right, what we could do better, what areas you'd like to see us publish in, and any other words of wisdom you're willing to pass our way.

You can email or write me directly to let me know what you did or didn't like about this book—as well as what we can do to make our books stronger.

Please note that I cannot help you with technical problems related to the topic of this book, and that due to the high volume of mail I receive, I might not be able to reply to every message.

When you write, please be sure to include this book's title and author as well as your name and phone number or email address. I will carefully review your comments and share them with the author and editors who worked on the book.

E-mail: opensource@samspublishing.com

Mail: Mark Taber
          Associate Publisher
          Sams Publishing
          800 East 96th Street
          Indianapolis, IN 46240 USA

Introduction

If MySQL is a foreign land, *MySQL Phrasebook* is a concise guide to successfully navigating its broad streets, hectic bazaars, and dark alleys. Whether you're a tourist, a regular visitor, or even a local day-tripping to an unknown locale, this Phrasebook will help you find your way.

MySQL Phrasebook is not a definitive guide to all aspects of MySQL. Instead, it provides examples of how to accomplish some of the most common tasks in MySQL. This core of practical knowledge is supported with

- Tips for enhancing daily use
- Examples of the concepts being discussed
- Terse references to essential MySQL tools and syntax
- References to more details and resources on MySQL

Omissions: What This Book Doesn't Cover

The Phrasebook aims to be compact, rather than comprehensive. As such, a few topics have been omitted:

- **Installation or configuration of MySQL**— This book assumes that your MySQL installation is already up and running.

- **MaxDB or MySQL Cluster**—Although much of the content in *MySQL Phrasebook* applies to these database engines, this book does not specifically describe their implementation or use.

- **Detailed coverage of features and functions**—This book is not a complete reference for MySQL and only provides the most essential information on major features and functions.

- **Advanced topics**—Advanced topics, such as debugging server crashes, tuning replication, and so on, are not discussed.

Conventions Used in This Book

This book uses several conventions with regard to using the command line that are important to understand.

Default Assumptions

If code is listed without a prompt, it is assumed to be SQL and can be run in any MySQL client.

shell>

The shell> prompt indicates that the text following the prompt should be entered in your system's shell (Unix) or command window (Windows).

mysql>

The mysql> prompt indicates that the text following the prompt should be entered in the mysql command-line client.

Whether entering commands at a shell prompt or within the MySQL command-line client, only enter the text that, in the book, follows the prompt. Do not enter the prompt itself.

The *MySQL Phrasebook* Website

The complete content of *MySQL Phrasebook* is available online at www.samspublishing.com/.

Maps of MySQL

MySQL and other Relational Database Management Systems (RDBMS) are complex pieces of software that consist of many components.

The maps provide a simplified view of how the various pieces of the system relate to each other and to common tasks. The maps are intended to help readers

- Understand the major logical components of MySQL and RDBMSs

- See how MySQL relates to its environment

- Easily find the right section of the guide

The MySQL RDBMS

MySQL RDBMS

A Simplified View

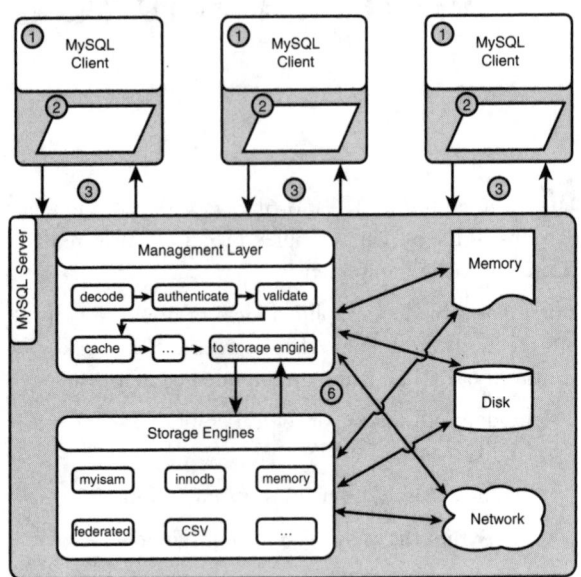

1. One or more MySQL clients connect to one (or more) MySQL servers.

2. Each client handles work such as

   - Initiating authentication, password hashing, and so forth

   - Reducing text queries into more efficient tokens

   - Delivering queries to the server

- Caching result sets from the server
- Managed compressed and/or encrypted connections

3. The MySQL server handles requests from clients and returns responses to them.

4. Requests are first handled by the management layer, which is the coordinator for the MySQL server. It handles tasks such as

   - Decrypting and/or decoding connections
   - Validating and parsing queries
   - Fetching cached queries from the query cache
   - Passing instructions to the correct storage engine

5. Storage engines manage the memory and disk-level representation of databases, tables, and indexes. Each storage engine manages different types of databases, tables, indexes, and so on. They also manage some logs and statistics generation.

6. The management layer and the storage engines interact heavily with the memory, the disk, and the network. The management layer writes logs to disk, stores and reads caches in memory, reads binary logs from the network, and so on. The storage engines store data (tables, logs, and so forth) on disk and in memory, sends data via the network to other remote MySQL servers, and so on.

MAPS OF MYSQL

The LAMP Platform

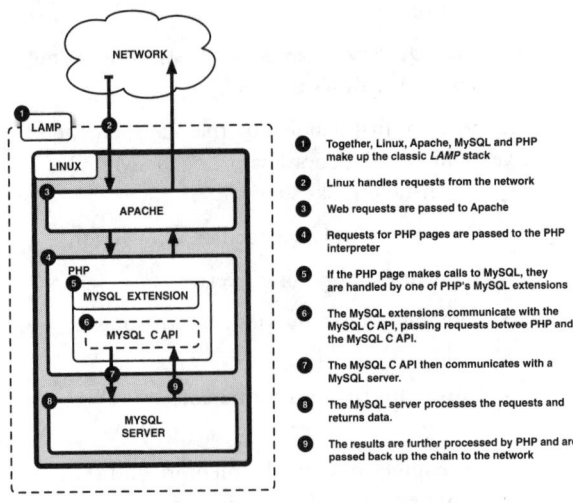

① Together, Linux, Apache, MySQL and PHP make up the classic *LAMP* stack

② Linux handles requests from the network

③ Web requests are passed to Apache

④ Requests for PHP pages are passed to the PHP interpreter

⑤ If the PHP page makes calls to MySQL, they are handled by one of PHP's MySQL extensions

⑥ The MySQL extensions communicate with the MySQL C API, passing requests betwee PHP and the MySQL C API.

⑦ The MySQL C API then communicates with a MySQL server.

⑧ The MySQL server processes the requests and returns data.

⑨ The results are further processed by PHP and are passed back up the chain to the network

MySQL Table Terminology

MySQL Table Terminology

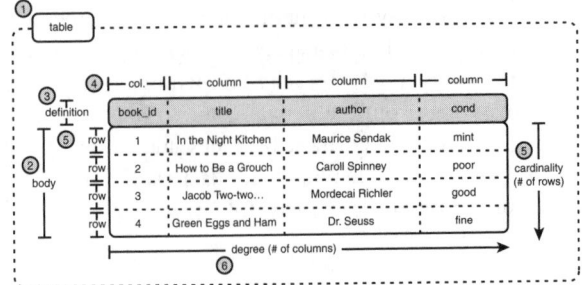

The components of a MySQL table are

1. A table is a structured collection of data, which is composed of...

2. a body, that contains rows of data and...

3. a table definition that contains columns that describe the type of data contained in the rows.

4. Each column has a name (such as book_id) and a type (such as INTEGER). Each type is a defined set of values (like integers or letters in the alphabet). If data is of a given type, it must be one of the values from that type (for example, a column with type INTEGER must contain a whole number value such as 1 or 6502, not a string value such as one or a decimal number such as 3.14).

5. Each row contains one value for every column in the heading. The values must be of the type defined in the column to which they correspond. The column book_id is of type SMALLINT—only values of that type may be stored in that position in the row.

6. The number of columns a relation has defines its *degree*.

7. The number of rows a relation has defines its *cardinality*.

Sample Tables

MySQL Phrasebook Sample Tables

Table: book

book_id	title	author	cond
1	In the Night Kitchen	Maurice Sendak	mint
2	How to Be a Grouch	Caroll Spinney	poor
3	Jacob Two-two...	Mordecai Richler	good
4	Green Eggs and Ham	Dr. Seuss	fine

Table: person

person_id	name	email
1	Yvette	yvette@example.com
2	Lenz	lenz@example.com
3	Thies	thies@example.com
4	Harmony	harmony@example.com

Table: loan

loan_id	book_id	person_id	date_lent
1	2	3	2005-07-17
2	3	3	2005-07-17
3	1	4	2005-09-10
4	4	1	2005-06-05
5	4	3	2005-10-18

Creating and Managing Databases, Tables, and Indexes

The phrases in this chapter focus on creating and managing the structures in MySQL that, from a logical point of view, store and organize the data that lives on the MySQL server.

Not all readers are familiar with the basics of how MySQL models the data that it stores, so we will also take a five-minute detour to discuss the basics of databases, tables, columns, and indexes.

Quick Guide: Databases, Tables, Columns, and Indexes

The basic model MySQL uses for structuring the data it stores is fairly simple to understand—but, perhaps, only when you already understand it. The basic model is as follows:

- The MySQL server contains one or more databases.

- Each database has a name and contains one or more tables.

- Each table has a name, a table definition, and zero or more rows.

- Each table definition specifies one or more columns for the table and zero or more indexes.

- Each column has a name and a defined column type.

- Column types are a predefined part of MySQL. Each one has a name and defines a list of values that columns of the given column type can contain.

- Each row in the table contains one value for every column in the table definition.

- Indexes reduce the effort it takes for the MySQL server to find a specific value in a specific column (or set of columns) of the table.

CHAPTER 2

> **TIP**
> Review the "MySQL Table Terminology" illustration in Chapter 1, "Maps of MySQL," to get a better feel for the discussion.

Databases are an easy concept to understand; they are just containers. Tables are a bit more difficult. Here is a simple metaphor to help you understand them.

A Simple Table Metaphor

A paper personal address book (the archetypical little black book) is a good rudimentary model for a database. Your simple version of the little black book contains pages where you can write information about friends or colleagues. Each entry for a person in the book is structured and contains a labeled space for the person's name, email address, and date of birth.

Additionally, each page is marked with an index tab to help you find people who are recorded in your book. Without the index tab, you have to look through the book until you find the person for whom you are looking.

Your book might look something like Figure 2.1.

Name: Mordecai Richler
Email: m.richler@example.com
DOB: 1931-1-27

Name:
Email:
R DOB:

Name:
Email:
DOB:

Name:
Email:
DOB:

Name: Maurice Sendak
Email: m.sendak@example.com
DOB: 1928-6-10

Name: Dr. Seuss
Email: dr.seuss@example.com
DOB: 1904-3-2

Name: Caroll Spinney
Email: c.spinney@example.com
DOB: 1933-12-26

Name:
Email:
DOB:

Figure 2.1 A personal address book.

Conceptually, the book can be thought of as a table of information that is composed of rows and columns.

Each row of the table refers to a single person, while each column in the table contains attributes about the person (such as name, email address, birthday, and so on.)

A tabular representation of the little black book is shown in Figure 2.2.

last name	first name	email	birthday
Sendak	Maurice	m.sendak@example.com	1928-06-10
Spinney	Caroll	c.spinney@example.com	1933-12-26
Richler	Mordecai	m.richler@example.com	1931-01-27
Seuss	Doctor	dr.seuss@example.com	1904-03-02

Figure 2.2   The personal address book as a table.

In your paper address book, you put a person on the page that is marked with the right index tab for the first letter of his last name. Maurice Sendak, for example, is put on the same page as index tab S.

In your table, rows are stored in an arbitrary order. To help you find the right row without having to scan through the database, columns in the table can have indexes. Conceptually, indexes are lists of sorted values from a column that are correlated to the actual position of the value in the column.

The diagram in Figure 2.3 illustrates how an index correlates to the actual position of rows in a table.

index by last name	last name	first name	email	birthday
Richler	Sendak	Maurice	m.sendak@example.com	1928-06-10
Sendak	Spinney	Caroll	c.spinney@example.com	1933-12-26
Seuss	Richler	Mordecai	m.richler@example.com	1931-01-27
Spinney	Seuss	Doctor	dr.seuss@example.com	1904-03-02

Figure 2.3   Actual position of rows in a table.

Creating and Managing Databases

Databases are, for the most part, easy to create and maintain—they are simple containers with few properties of their own. The following phrases cover most of what you will need to know for creating, maintaining, and deleting them.

List All Databases

```
SHOW DATABASES;
```

Use the SHOW DATABASES command to fetch a list of the names of the databases on the MySQL server to which you are connected.

On a new installation of MySQL, the SHOW DATABASES command might return a result like the following:

```
+----------+
| Database |
+----------+
| mysql    |
| test     |
+----------+
2 rows in set (0.00 sec)
```

Get a Filtered List of Databases

```
SHOW DATABASES LIKE 'my%';
```

If you only want to list database names that match all or part of a word, use the LIKE operator.

The word used with the LIKE operator is just a normal word, except that percent (%) and underscore (_) characters have a special meaning within the word. In the context of LIKE, percent (%) can represent any sequence of zero or more characters, while the underscore (_) wildcard can match any single character.

In this example, only databases whose names are my or start with my will be returned by SHOW DATABASES.

> **TIP**
>
> The LIKE operator can be used with many other SQL commands, including other SHOW commands and the WHERE clause of SELECT and DELETE commands.

If you are working with a newly installed copy of MySQL and run the sample code at the start of this phrase, you should see a result like the following:

```
+----------+
| Database |
+----------+
| mysql    |
+----------+
1 rows in set (0.00 sec)
```

NOTE

For more information on the LIKE operator, visit
http://mysql.com/LIKE.

Setting the Default Database

```
USE test;
```

A single installation of MySQL can have multiple databases. Any query that operates on a database or table
must have some way of knowing on which database or
table to operate. You can explicitly specify the database
to use within a query. For example, this query will be
made on the book table within the library database:

```
SELECT title FROM library.book;
```

Alternately, you can specify a default database to operate on with the USE command:

```
USE library;
```

Over time this can save quite a bit of typing because
after setting a default database, you no longer need to
explicitly specify the database in each query. The database specified in the USE command will be used by
default.

Compare the following queries. While the first and
third queries generate the same output, the first uses an
explicit database and the third uses the default database
specified by the second query.

```
SELECT title FROM library.book;
USE library;
SELECT title FROM book;
```

TIP

Even if a default database has been selected with the USE command, you can still explicitly specify a database to operate on within a given query (as in the first query above).

Creating a Database

```
CREATE DATABASE library;
```

This command creates a new database named library. On its own, the database isn't very useful. See the "Creating and Managing Tables" section to learn how to add tables to a database.

Deleting a Database

```
DROP DATABASE library;
```

The DROP DATABASE command removes a database, including all tables within the database.

CAUTION

Use DROP DATABASE very carefully—there is no way to easily undo the command after it has been executed.

Renaming a Database

Databases are not commonly renamed. In part, this is because performing the operation correctly is a little tricky. Additionally, there is no single SQL command within MySQL to rename databases.

In very old versions of MySQL, renaming a database was as simple a process as

1. Stopping the MySQL server
2. Renaming the directory that represented the database
3. Restarting the server

In modern versions of MySQL, this might cause the server to no longer recognize certain kinds of tables that were stored within the database. To safely rename a database, follow this process:

1. Ensure that none of the tables in the database are being accessed. A simple way to do this is to revoke all permissions to use the database. Use the MySQL Administrator tool to do so. See "Tailoring User Permissions" and "Removing User Access" in Chapter 6, "User Management and Security," for details.

2. Create a new database. Give it the name you want the old database to have.

3. For every table in the old database, use the SHOW TABLES and RENAME TABLE commands to move the table to the new database.

4. Give all users of the old database similar permissions on the new database.

5. Test to ensure that everything still works.

6. After you are sure everything works, delete the old database.

The code for migrating tables book, borrower, and loan from database books to database library might look like this:

```
-- Temporarily disable permissions
CREATE DATABASE library;
RENAME TABLE books.book TO library.book;
RENAME TABLE books.borrower TO library.borrower;
RENAME TABLE books.loan TO library.loan;
-- Migrate permissions
-- Re-enable permissions
```

Creating and Managing Tables

Tables are more complex structures than databases and (not surprisingly) take more work to create and manage.

These phrases focus on the basics that you need to survive. As there are literally hundreds of options available when creating tables, you will need additional resources to handle more complex tasks, such as setting the default collation for a column or defining tables that will store many terabytes of data.

Listing Some or All Tables in a Database

```
SHOW TABLES;
SHOW TABLES IN database_name;
SHOW TABLES LIKE 'word%';
SHOW TABLES IN database_name LIKE 'word%';
```

The first form of the SHOW TABLES command lists all tables in the default database, while the second command allows you to list the tables stored in a specific database. The third and fourth versions of the command show how the LIKE operator can be used with the command.

> **TIP**
>
> As with SHOW DATABASES, you can use the LIKE operator to restrict the list of tables shown by the SHOW TABLES command. See the "Get a Filtered List of Databases" phrase earlier in this chapter for more information on LIKE.

Creating Tables

```
CREATE TABLE book (
   id      SMALLINT UNSIGNED AUTO_INCREMENT NOT NULL,
   title   VARCHAR(255) NOT NULL,
   author  VARCHAR(255) NOT NULL,
   cond    ENUM('poor','good','fine','mint') NOT NULL,
           PRIMARY KEY (book_id),
);
```

Creating tables is a complex topic for two reasons: First, the syntax for creating tables is complex and consists of many elements. Second, the process of choosing how to create the table is even more complex.

Rather than attempt to cover either topic here, a simple example will remind you of what you either know or need to learn. You can refer to the online manual for the full syntax of these commands.

Renaming Tables

```
RENAME TABLE old_name TO new_name;
```

The syntax for renaming a table is simple and direct.

Tip

When renaming tables, keep in mind that there might still be users or applications that expect the table to be available under the old name. Use the phrase "Finding Users of a Given Database or Table" in Chapter 6 to spot possible problems.

Deleting Tables

```
DROP TABLE table_name;
```

Dropping a table means that, except for copies and backups, the table is gone for good. Use the command with caution.

TIP

Unless storage is an issue, rename tables instead of deleting them. After a few weeks or so, when you are sure that there are no problems, actually delete the table.

Copying Tables

```
CREATE TABLE new_table LIKE old_table;
INSERT new_table SELECT * FROM old_table;
```

Copies of existing tables come in very handy when testing destructive queries, installing a new instance of a database-centric application, or so on.

A variety of methods are available for making copies. The two queries in this phrase (when used together) create a complete copy of the structure and data of a table, complete with indexes, table options, and so on.

TIP

There are other ways to copy tables; however, they might be more dangerous, faster, specific to a certain type of table, less complete in what they copy, or a combination of these factors.

You can easily copy a table from one database to another by specifying the database name before the table name. For example:

```
CREATE TABLE db1.table LIKE db2.table;
INSERT db1.table SELECT * FROM db2.table;
```

The LIKE operator used in this query does not have the same meaning as the LIKE operator used in WHERE clauses and SHOW queries.

Creating and Managing Columns

Columns are usually created when a table is created. As application needs change, however, it is not uncommon to add a column or change how it is defined.

Even trivial modifications to a column will cause a table to be rebuilt. Always have backups before changing a column. For multi-gigabyte tables, the rebuild might take a significant amount of time. Consider making the change during a period of downtime or on a copy of the table.

Adding Columns

```
ALTER TABLE table_name
     ADD COLUMN [column_definition];
ALTER TABLE book
     ADD COLUMN ISBN VARCHAR(10) NOT NULL;
```

Columns can easily be added to existing tables.

Take a column definition that is appropriate for a CREATE TABLE statement and prepend ALTER TABLE table_name COLUMN to it.

The first query shows the general form of the query. The second query shows a specific example of the query, where an ISBN column is being added to a book table.

Changing Column Definitions (and Names)

```
ALTER TABLE table_name
     CHANGE COLUMN column_name [column_definition];
ALTER TABLE book
     CHANGE COLUMN ISBN isbn VARCHAR(10) NOT NULL;
```

Changing the definition of a column (including giving a column a new name) is similar to the process of adding a column. There is a minor difference in syntax: Use ALTER TABLE ... CHANGE COLUMN instead of ALTER TABLE ... ADD COLUMN. The column definition must contain the column name before its type and attributes, so if you are changing the definition of a column but not its name, the column name appears twice in the statement.

The first query shows the general syntax for the query, while the second query shows a specific query where you change the name and width of the ISBN column of the book table.

Deleting Columns

```
ALTER TABLE table_name DROP COLUMN column_name;
```

Deleting a column from a table is a simple process. Keep in mind the usual caveats about commands that delete things from the database: You can't undo the deletion, and people might depend on the thing you are deleting.

TIP
Deleting a column also deletes any indexes that include that column.

Identifiers

MySQL identifiers, such as database and column names, are case sensitive under most circumstances. To keep things simple, it is best to always use lowercase for these identifiers. To force MySQL to behave consistently across all platforms, set the lower_case_table_names configuration variable to 1. This forces all case-sensitive identifiers to be treated as lowercase. For more information on identifier names, see the MySQL manual at http://mysql.com/identifier case sensitivity.

Creating and Managing Indexes

Indexes are often the most significant factor affecting how rapidly data can (or cannot) be retrieved from large tables.

This section provides the basic details on how to manage indexes—it does not cover the topic of how to choose which columns to index or how indexes are used. For more information, read Chapter 4, "Retrieving Data: Simple Queries."

Adding an Index to a Table

```
CREATE INDEX index_name
       ON table_name (column_name, ...);
CREATE INDEX author ON book (author);
CREATE INDEX author ON book (author(16));
CREATE INDEX title_author ON book (title, author);
```

To add an index to a set of columns in an existing table, you use the CREATE INDEX command (or the ALTER TABLE command, but this book covers CREATE INDEX, as it is easier to remember).

The command requires that you specify a name for the new index along with the name of the table in which to create the index and the column (or columns) on which to create the index.

The first query shows a generic form of the command, where you would need to include your own specific values. The remaining queries show specific examples that add various indexes to the book table.

Renaming an Index

Renaming indexes is done infrequently. An index is usually simply deleted or its definition changed. If you do want to rename an index, delete the index and re-create it.

Deleting an Index

```
DROP INDEX index_name ON table_name;
DROP INDEX author ON book;
```

The syntax for deleting an index is very simple—you merely state which index to remove from which table.

The first query shows the generic form of the query. The second query deletes an index called author from a table called book.

See Also

The following sections of the online reference manual provide more information about the topics covered in this chapter:

- **Data Definition Statements**—http://dev.mysql.com/doc/refman/5.0/en/data-definition.html

- **How MySQL Uses Indexes**—http://dev.mysql.com/doc/refman/5.0/en/mysql-indexes.html

CREATING AND MANAGING DATABASES, TABLES, AND INDEXES

3

Storing Data

This chapter covers the basics of the SQL and MySQL commands that are used for getting data into a table. It doesn't cover topics such as programmatically adding data to a table (see Chapter 8, "MySQL APIs") or updating data already in a table (see Chapter 5, "Manipulating Data").

Adding Data to a Table

```
# Generic syntax
INSERT table_name (list, of, columns)
VALUES (list, of, values);

# Add one row to the book table
INSERT book (title, author, cond)
VALUES ('Where the Wild Things Are',
        'Maurice Sendak',
        'fine');
```

The INSERT command allows you to add one or more rows to an existing table. The basic syntax of the command is quite simple. Piece-by-piece, the relevant bits of syntax are

- **INSERT**—Denotes the start of the command.
- *table_name*—The name of an existing table (such as book) to insert one or more rows of data into.
- **(*list, of, columns*, ...)**—A parenthesized list of column names. Columns not included in this list will be set to their default values in the rows that will be created.

> **TIP**
>
> The list of columns is optional. If it is omitted, it will be as if all columns were listed. Use of this behavior, however, is not at all recommended because the order of columns in a table cannot be trusted to remain consistent over time.

- **VALUES**—Lets MySQL know that a list of values should be coming next.
- **(*list, of, values*, ...)**—A parenthesized list of values that should correspond to the list of columns specified.

> **TIP**
>
> Note that not only values can be used in the list—function calls, variables, and other exciting things are allowed as well. See the "Inserting the Current Date and Time (Using a MySQL Function)" phrase later in this chapter.

Adding Many Rows in One Query Using INSERT

```
INSERT book (author, title, cond)
  VALUES
    ('Maurice Sendak',
     'In the Night Kitchen','mint'),
    ('Caroll Spinney','How to Be a Grouch','poor'),
    ('Dr. Seuss', 'Green Eggs and Ham', 'good');
```

The INSERT command can insert many rows in a single query by using multiple lists of values. Each set of values should be enclosed in parenthesis and separated by a comma. Place a semicolon after the final value list.

In addition to reducing the amount of typing that needs to be done, inserting multiple rows of data with a single SQL query has the advantage of efficiency: MySQL has to do less work than if it had to process three separate queries.

Assigning Unique Row Numbers with auto_increment

```
CREATE TABLE table (
  column INT AUTO_INCREMENT,
  ...
);
```

AUTO_INCREMENT columns provide a way to automatically number rows in a table. Every time a new row is inserted into a table, a value equal to one (unless another value is specified for the AUTO_INCREMENT columns) plus the largest value stored in that AUTO_INCREMENT column will be inserted into the column. Alternately, insert a NULL into the column to get the same effect. Using a NULL lets others who read the code after you know that you explicitly want the column to auto-increment.

Examine and run the following sample code for a tangible demonstration of auto-incrementing:

```
CREATE TEMPORARY TABLE demo (
  id INT NOT NULL AUTO_INCREMENT,
    PRIMARY KEY (id)
);
INSERT demo () VALUES ();
SELECT id FROM demo; # id contains 1
INSERT demo (id) VALUES (NULL);
SELECT id FROM demo; # id contains 1 and 2
INSERT demo (id) VALUES (4);
SELECT id FROM demo; # id contains 1, 2 and 4
INSERT demo (id) VALUES (NULL);
SELECT id FROM demo; # id contains 1, 2, 4
    and 5
```

Note that there can only be one AUTO_INCREMENT column for a table and that it must be a part of the primary key.

When you delete rows in a table that has an AUTO_INCREMENT column, you will likely have gaps in the sequence of numbers in the column. Unless you are in the situation where the value inserted into the AUTO_INCREMENT column is approaching the maximum value that can be stored in the column—more than 2 billion for an INT column—don't worry about this. It might seem ugly, but not re-using the same number for different rows helps ensure that your data remain consistent.

If you are close to running out of space on the column, change the type of the column to one that can

hold larger values before renumbering the AUTO_
INCREMENT sequence.

Inserting the Current Date and Time (Using a MySQL Function)

```
INSERT some_table (some_column) VALUES (NOW());
```

The above snippet of SQL uses a MySQL function
(called NOW()) to insert the current date and time into
fictional column *some_column* in fictional table
some_table.

When NOW() is called, it returns the current date and
time (with a precision of seconds) on the machine on
which the MySQL server is running. By default, the
function returns the text in a human-friendly format,
with spaces and punctuation to help readability (such
as 2005-09-04 01:43:37). Run SELECT NOW(); for a
sample.

If you would like to have the date and time shown as
just a string of numbers (such as 20050904014624), add
zero to the value of NOW(). Your statement will look
like SELECT NOW()+0;

TIP

Many useful functions and operators are included with
MySQL that allow you to perform mathematical operations, generate conditional output based on the comparison of a column and a value, and so on. For more
information, see the online manual.

Loading SQL Commands from a File

```
shell> mysql -u username -p db_name < file_name.sql
mysql> \. file_name.sql
```

Most of the phrases in this book assume that you are interactively entering commands into mysql, the MySQL command-line client. You can, however, just as easily store the commands in plain text files and then use mysql (or some other client) to run the commands.

In the first example, you are running mysql in batch mode on the command line. In batch mode, mysql runs one or more commands, displays output (if any), and then exits.

More specifically, in the first example, mysql

1. Connects to the MySQL server using the specified *username*

2. Prompts for a password to attempt to authenticate with

3. Sets the default database to be *db_name*

4. Sends the contents of *file_name.sql* to the server

5. Displays the results (if any) of the command

6. Exits

In the second example, the contents of file *file_name.sql* are read in by the client and sent to the server. The important things to note are that you are already using the mysql command-line client in interactive mode.

Inserting Data from Another Table

```
# General syntax for INSERT ... SELECT
INSERT table_one (list, of, columns) SELECT ...;
```

The INSERT command can be combined with a SELECT command to allow easy copying of rows from one table to another table.

The syntax is very simple. Take the front part of the INSERT command (up to the VALUES clause) and graft a SELECT command to it. Just make sure that the SELECT returns one column for every column that the INSERT command requires.

This example shows the general syntax for the INSERT ... SELECT command. For a more complex example that demonstrates a practical use of this feature, see phrase "Splitting a Column into Its Own Table" in Chapter 5, "Manipulating Data."

Importing Data from Text Files

```
LOAD DATA INFILE 'some_file.txt'
    INTO TABLE 'some_table' (list, of, columns, ...);
```

STORING DATA

Migrating data between other applications and MySQL is often easiest done by exporting the data to a structured text format (such as tab-separated values) and then importing it into MySQL.

The import could be done by converting the data into a set of SQL queries, but this approach can be cumbersome and error-prone. A simpler (and much faster) method for getting data from structured text files into MySQL is to use the LOAD DATA INFILE command.

By default, LOAD DATA INFILE understands how to import files that are in a tab-separated value format, where each field in the file is separated by a tab and each row by a newline.

When LOAD DATA INFILE reads a row from the data file, it adds a row to the target table using the column mapping specified.

For example, you want to import the following text file into your book table:

```
Where the Wild Things Are→Maurice Sendak→fine
Cigars of the Pharoah→Herge→good
...→...→...
```

If this file is saved to /Users/zak/books_and_authors. txt, you can import the text using the following command:

```
USE library;
LOAD DATA INFILE '/Users/zak/books_and_authors.txt'
  INTO TABLE book (title, author, cond);
```

This should result in table book containing the following new rows:

```
+---------+---------------+----------------+------+
| book_id | title         | author         | cond |
+---------+---------------+----------------+------+
|       5 | Cigars of ... | Herge          | good |
|       6 | Where the ... | Maurice Sendak | fine |
|       7 | ...           | ...            | ...  |
+---------+---------------+----------------+------+
```

There are a few key things to note in the LOAD DATA
INFILE command:

- The data file is stored on the same machine as the
  MySQL server.

TIP

If you are working with a remote MySQL server and want
to load data from a local file to the server, you need to
use the LOCAL keyword. Visit http://mysql.com/LOAD DATA
INFILE for more information.

- You need to specify the complete path to the file
  from which you load data. If you just specify a
  filename without a path, the MySQL server will
  look somewhere in its data directory. If you are
  using the LOCAL keyword and do not specify a full
  path, the MySQL client will look in the directory
  from which it was started.

- On Windows systems, you should still use forward
  slashes in your path (instead of backslashes). For
  example, on a Windows system, the Unix-style
  path used ('/Users/zak/books_and_authors.txt')
  might instead be 'C:/Desktop/book_and_authors.
  txt'. If backslashes had been used in the previous
  path, they would be interpreted as character
  escape sequences.

Additionally, here are a few general tips to make your use of LOAD DATA INFILE easier:

- If the output of the command is followed by a warning or error (such as Query OK, 3 rows affected, 1 warning (0.01 sec)), use SHOW WARNINGS; or SHOW ERRORS; to display the exact problems that were encountered.

- To test if you have set up a complex LOAD DATA INFILE correctly, create a temporary table like the table with which you plan to work. Then run your LOAD DATA INFILE command on the temporary table instead. If necessary for performance or storage reasons, limit the amount of data that you load into the temporary table. For example, if you had wanted to test the code in this example before letting it near your production database, you could have used the following code:

```
USE library;

# Create a temp table like your real table
CREATE TEMPORARY TABLE book_temp LIKE book;

# load in part of your data
LOAD DATA INFILE
'/Users/zak/books_and_authors.txt'
  INTO TABLE book_temp (title, author, cond)
  IGNORE 195 LINES;
  # ignore the first 195 lines

SELECT * FROM book_temp;
# see if things look ok
```

- The command has many options to allow you to control how data is imported, such as what format of data is read, how many rows are imported, and so on. See http://mysql.com/LOAD DATA INFILE for more information.

Inserting Data Rapidly

If you frequently have many rows of data to insert into a table and find that performance starts to be an issue, here are some tips to help. First, there are different techniques to use depending on if you are inserting many rows at once or inserting many rows over a period of time but have many reads interspersed with the writes.

For inserting many rows of data at once, try these optimizations:

- If possible, use LOAD DATA INFILE (see the phrase "Importing Data from Text Files" in this chapter). It provides a performance benefit by reducing the amount of work that both the client and server must do to prepare the data for insertion into a table.

- Use the ALTER TABLE command to temporarily disable index creation when inserting large amounts of data. This allows the work of building the table indexes to be done in one efficient step after the data is inserted. For example:

```
ALTER TABLE table_name DISABLE KEYS;
# Many INSERT statements here
ALTER TABLE table_name ENABLE KEYS;
```

- For MyISAM tables, lock the table while inserting data to prevent reads from the table from slowing down the writes. You can use the following code:

```
LOCK TABLES table_name WRITE;
# Many INSERT statements here
UNLOCK TABLES;
```

- For InnoDB tables, run all of your INSERT statements within a transaction with the following code:

```
BEGIN;
# Many INSERT statements here
COMMIT;
```

- Use a multivalue INSERT. These types of statements reduce the amount of work that the client and server must do to process a query before the data is written to a table. See the phrase "Adding Many Rows in One Query Using INSERT" in this chapter.

For inserting many rows of data interspersed with many reads, try these optimizations:

- For MyISAM tables, enable the DELAY_KEY_WRITE table option. This option reduces the number of disk writes that MySQL has to make when creating new entries in a table's index. You can set the option on an existing table using ALTER TABLE as in the following code:

```
ALTER TABLE table_name DELAY_KEY_WRITE = 1;
```

CAUTION

If the MySQL server crashes, tables that have DELAY_KEY_WRITE set might have incomplete indexes. To ensure that the indexes are complete, you should restart the MySQL server with --myisam-recover=BACKUP,FORCE.

- Use InnoDB tables. They handle many concurrent reads and writes better than MyISAM tables.

- Don't write to the table you read from. Instead, create a table for handling writes and then merge the rows from the write table into your read table at a regular interval using the bulk insert tips mentioned previously to get better performance.

There are many additional ways to squeeze performance out of MySQL. Some options include hardware configuration choices, server configuration, table design, SQL optimizations, and so on. For more information, refer to the online manual.

See Also

The following sections of the online reference manual provide more information about the topics covered in this chapter:

- **Data Manipulation Statements**—http:// dev.mysql.com/doc/refman/5.0/en/ data-manipulation.html

- **Using AUTO_INCREMENT**—http://dev.mysql.com/ doc/refman/5.0/en/example-auto-increment.html

4

Retrieving Data: Simple Queries

This chapter covers the basic phrases needed to survive your first few days with MySQL. Phrases for some of the most common tasks, such as sorting data or finding text that matches a particular pattern, are provided, and finding your way out of a few major pitfalls, such as the mysterious and perplexing NULL, is discussed.

For more advanced queries, including joins and subqueries, see Chapter 9, "Advanced Queries."

Limiting the Number of Rows Returned

```
# Use the LIMIT clause to fetch the first two rows
SELECT author FROM book LIMIT 2;

# ... or starting from the second row, fetch two
# rows
SELECT author FROM book LIMIT 1, 2;
```

The LIMIT clause is used to fetch a limited subset of rows from a query. The clause can be used in two ways. You can either

- Fetch the first n rows from a query, as is shown in the first example in the phrasebox. The syntax is LIMIT n, where n is some integer number.

- Fetch a range of rows, as is shown in the second phrasebox example. The syntax for this use of LIMIT is LIMIT x, y. In this use, the clause causes the query to return y rows, starting from the xth row.

CHAPTER 4

> **NOTE**
>
> The counting of rows (at least for the purpose of LIMIT) begins with zero, not one. For example, to grab rows 12 through 15 of a query, you would say SELECT * FROM *some_table* LIMIT 11, 4;.

The practical uses of LIMIT will be covered in more detail in phrase "Paging Through a Result Set" in Chapter 8, "MySQL APIs."

Sorting Result Sets

```
# Get a list of alphabetically sorted book names
SELECT title FROM book ORDER BY title;

# Sort alphabetically but with an exception
SELECT name FROM status
  ORDER BY name='default' DESC, name;
```

When you fetch rows from MySQL, they are returned to you in a haphazard order that might or might not fit your needs. Thankfully, MySQL allows you to specify in which order the rows should be returned.

The order is specified using the ORDER BY clause. The clause accepts a list of one or more expressions (which can just be column names). For every row, the expressions in the ORDER BY clause are evaluated. Then the resulting values are put into a list that is then sorted. The rows are then returned according to this order.

Sound complex? Here is a simplified version of the steps laid out for you:

1. A query is sent to the server, like so:

    ```
    SELECT * FROM book ORDER BY title;
    ```

2. For every row that is returned, the appropriate value of the `title` column is put into a list, like the following:

    ```
    Green Eggs and Ham (Row 1)
    In the Night Kitchen (Row 2)
    How to Be a Grouch (Row 3)
    Jacob Two-Two Meets the Hooded Fang (Row 4)
    ```

    Additionally, the server knows to which row the title corresponds.

3. The list is sorted alphabetically and is not case-sensitive, but you can specify other types of sorting, if you want:

    ```
    Green Eggs and Ham (Row 1)
    How to Be a Grouch (Row 3)
    In the Night Kitchen (Row 2)
    Jacob Two-Two Meets the Hooded Fang (Row 4)
    ```

4. The rows are returned in the same order as the sorted list.

RETRIEVING DATA: SIMPLE QUERIES

Ignoring Duplicate Rows

```
# Fetch only unique last names from a
# phone book
SELECT DISTINCT surnames FROM phonebook;
```

Some queries might return duplicate rows of data. This might happen when selecting just the last names of people listed in a phone book. If you used a simple query of

```
SELECT surnames FROM phonebook;
```

you would likely have thousands of duplicated rows for common names such as Moore, Johnston, and Smith.

If you place the DISTINCT clause after the SELECT, multiple values are returned only once.

When the query selects more than one column, DISTINCT only removes duplicate rows where every column value is identical.

Finding Text That Matches a Pattern

```
# Find simple patterns with the LIKE operator
SELECT name FROM author WHERE name LIKE 'M%';
```

MySQL provides many ways to find text that matches a specific pattern (*pattern* means something such as "All names that start with M" or "All names where the surname is six or more letters long"). One of the most commonly used and useful pattern-matching tools is the LIKE operator.

LIKE allows you to match text against simple patterns that can include these two wildcard characters: percent (%) and underscore (_):

- % matches zero or more characters of any type.
- _ matches exactly one character of any type.

For example, if you want to find all author names that start with M and are at least six characters long, you would type

```
SELECT name FROM author
WHERE name LIKE 'M_____%';
```

For example, if you want to find all author names that end in the letter k, you would type

```
SELECT name FROM author WHERE name LIKE '%k';
```

CAUTION

Queries that use LIKE patterns that begin with a wildcard cannot use indexes. Beware of this and try to avoid running repetitive queries that use this technique.

TIP

To match a literal % or _ within the context of LIKE, prefix the wildcard with a backslash, as shown in the following:

```
SELECT * FROM some_table
    WHERE some_column LIKE '__\%';
```

To find all text that does not match a given LIKE pattern, precede LIKE with NOT, as in the following:

```
SELECT name FROM author
    WHERE name NOT LIKE 'M%';
```

For more information on the various string-matching functions, refer to

- All MySQL string-comparison functions, including C-like functions such as `strstr()`:

  http://dev.mysql.com/doc/refman/5.0/en/string-comparison-functions.html

- MySQL's full-text indexes, which allow rapid development of a search engine–like functionality within a MySQL application:

  http://mysql.com/fulltext

- Examples of using the complex, powerful (and slow) regular expression function:

  http://mysql.com/regex

Finding the Smallest, Largest, or Average Value in a Column

```
# Find the minimum, maximum, and average weights
SELECT MIN(wt), AVG(wt), MAX(wt) FROM person;
```

MySQL provides a variety of functions to perform basic grouping or math on column values. These functions range from grouping functions such as `MIN()` and `MAX()`, to simple calculations such as `AVG()`, all the way to statistical and trigonometric functions.

`MIN()` and `MAX()`, respectively, return the minimum and maximum values stored in a given column, while `AVG()` returns the average of all values in the column as a floating point number.

Interestingly, `MIN()` and `MAX()` work with columns that contain text. `MIN()` returns the value that would come first alphabetically, while MAX() returns the value that would come last alphabetically.

For more information on the various mathematical and grouping functions, see the MySQL online manual, in particular these sections:

- http://dev.mysql.com/doc/refman/5.0/en/ group-by-functions-and-modifiers.html

- http://dev.mysql.com/doc/refman/5.0/en/ mathematical-functions.html

Date and Time Manipulation

```
# Find dates newer than one week ago
SELECT users FROM accounts
  WHERE created >=
        DATE_SUB(CURDATE(), INTERVAL 1 WEEK);
```

Basic manipulations and comparisons of dates and times within MySQL are quite simple.

MySQL allows date and time information to be conveniently represented in the international format of 'YYYY-MM-DD HH:MM:SS' (for example, '2005-09-30 18:43:01') or a more compact representation of YYYYMMDDHHMMSS (for example, 20050930184301).

A variety of useful functions, such as DATE_ADD() or DATE_SUB(), can be used to add and subtract dates and times, extract fragments such as hours or year from a date/time, and so on.

Additionally, the standard mathematical comparison operators of greater than (>), less than (<), equivalence (=), and so on, can be used to compare dates to each other.

Some of the most commonly used parts of MySQL's date and time functionality are the NOW(), CURDATE(), and CURTIME() functions. CURDATE() returns the current date, while, not surprisingly, CURTIME() returns the current time. NOW() returns both the current date and time.

In the phrasebox sample, the greater-than-or-equals operator (>=) is used in conjunction with CURDATE() and DATE_SUB() to find all users in a fictional accounts table who were created between now and the past week. In this case, you assume that the created column contains dates.

Most manipulations of date and time are simple enough and behave as expected. However, beware of time zones, daylight savings time, calendar changes for historical dates, wandering system clocks, two-digit century representations, overly short timestamps, and other fearsome beasts as you design any program that deals with dates and times on a larger scale.

A few simple tips to help keep you out of trouble are

- Use Network Time Protocol (NTP) to keep your computer's time up-to-date.

- When possible, use more precision than you need to store your dates.

- If you need to be precise about times, store them in Coordinated Universal Time (UTC), also known as Greenwich Mean Time (GMT), and then add logic in your programs to display the appropriate local time for users.

For more information on working with dates and times, see the MySQL online manual, these sections in particular:

- http://dev.mysql.com/doc/refman/5.0/en/date-and-time-type-overview.html

- http://dev.mysql.com/doc/refman/5.0/en/date-and-time-functions.html

Storing Exact Floating Point Numbers

Within MySQL, most floating point numbers are represented in a compact, but inaccurate, format. If this sounds terrible, it is—but on the bright side, MySQL shares this problem with the rest of the computing world.

One partial exception to this behavior comes in the form of the DECIMAL-type column. DECIMAL columns store floating point numbers as strings, instead of as floating point numbers. This approach requires more space, but you can be sure of the level of precision in the data that you store in MySQL. Of course, there is a limit to how much data is in the DECIMAL column. The limit for the amount of data that can be stored has changed several times in recent versions of MySQL, so check the MySQL manual for more details. To be compatible with all released versions of MySQL, limit the number of digits to the right of the decimals to 30 or fewer.

DECIMAL is handled just like other column types. See Chapter 2, "Creating and Managing Databases, Tables, and Indexes," for more details.

> **TIP**
>
> If you do math on a DECIMAL-type column within MySQL, you face a loss in precision unless you are using MySQL version 5.0.3 or greater.

Dealing with NULL

```
# Matching NULL
SELECT id FROM author WHERE name IS NULL;

# Using the NULL-safe equality operator
SELECT * FROM some_table
WHERE NOT some_column <=> 1;
```

NULL is a tricky little bit of SQL syntax that stands in for nothing. Note that nothing is not the same as empty or zero. This distinction leads to a good deal of confusion when dealing with NULL. For example, try running the following snippets of SQL in MySQL:

```
SELECT NULL = FALSE;
SELECT NULL = '';
SELECT NULL = 0;
SELECT NULL = NULL;
```

The result of all of these queries is NULL. NULL does not have a value—by definition it means there is no value—and it has no data type. It is therefore not equal to a Boolean FALSE, an empty string, or an integer zero. When you compare NULL to another value, however, the result is always NULL, not FALSE or zero. Furthermore, NULL does not equal NULL, as the previous comparison shows.

If you are working with a column that contains NULL values, keep these things in mind:

- If you try to compare anything to NULL using the standard comparison operators, the comparison returns NULL. The practical effect of this is that queries such as the following always return no rows:

```
SELECT * FROM some_table
WHERE some_column != NULL;
```

- Use the special NULL-safe operators IS NULL and <=> to safely compare anything to a NULL.

Sending Query Results to a File

```
# Dump a query as comma-separated values
SELECT * FROM author
  INTO OUTFILE '/tmp/author'
    FIELDS TERMINATED BY ','
    ENCLOSED BY '"'
    LINES TERMINATED BY '\n';
```

RETRIEVING DATA: SIMPLE QUERIES

If desired, you can quickly write a table out to a file on disk using the INTO OUTFILE clause of the SELECT statement. The default behavior of the clause, when used in its simplest form of SELECT ... INTO OUTFILE '/some/file/name', is to write out the file in tab-separated value format, with each field separated by a tab and each row separated by a newline.

INTO OUTFILE can accept additional options to control the format of the file that is written. The example query in the phrasebox outputs one style of comma-separated value (CSV) file.

The options are fairly self-explanatory for experienced programmers but might be a little baffling for novices. The important thing to remember is that character sequences such as '\n' and '\t' have a special meaning—instead of representing a literal backslash followed by a lower case n or t, they are interpreted by MySQL to mean newline or tab.

For more detailed information on how to control the format of the file generated, see the SELECT page of the MySQL online manual (http://mysql.com/select).

Writing a BLOB to a File

```
SELECT data FROM some_table
    WHERE name="img12"
    INTO DUMPFILE "/tmp/img12.jpg";
```

If you have stored binary data from a file in a BLOB column within a table and want to reconstitute it into a file, use the INTO DUMPFILE clause of the SELECT statement. INTO DUMPFILE writes data from a query directly to a file without modifying it in any way.

INTO DUMPFILE only works with SELECT statements that return a single row. If multiple columns are in the row, they are concatenated together without any separator. For example,

```
SELECT 1, 2, 3, 4 INTO DUMPFILE '/tmp/numbers';
```

creates a file that contains 1234.

Manipulating Data

Prices go up. People move. Companies merge. Overpasses need to be built. Life changes and the data in a database must be updated to reflect this. Additionally, sometimes design choices for tables and databases might need to be rethought, requiring changes to both the data and the structures in which the data is stored.

The phrases in this chapter focus on the hows and whys of changing data that is already stored within MySQL tables, with a little bit of changing MySQL tables thrown in for good measure.

Safety Tips

There is no undo feature in MySQL. If you issue a query such as DROP DATABASE test, all of the tables stored in test are instantly deleted. If this query was issued by mistake, you can only recover the data from logs, from backups, or (in some instances) by using a data recovery tool.

Here are a few tips to help you work more safely with your MySQL databases. Most of these tips are geared for data on the scale of thousands of rows making up tens of megabytes in size or less. For larger installations, get expert help!

- Don't grant users (including yourself) more permissions than they need. For example, if you are running some ad hoc queries on a database for the finance department, don't use the MySQL root account. Instead, create a user who only has permission to run the needed SELECT queries and then log in as that user. This might seem paranoid, but it can save a lot of hassle in the long run. For more on managing users and accounts, see Chapter 6, "User Management and Security."

- Keep up-to-date backups. Although the topic of backups is outside of the scope of this book, it is important that your server administrator keep daily backups of the data stored in MySQL.

- Make ad hoc backups as needed. Even if your system administrator does make frequent backups of MySQL, there might be times when you want to make your own backup of the data. Consider making your own backup before you make any radical changes to the data or when you are using unfamiliar features. See Chapter 10, "Troubleshooting and Emergencies," to learn how to use the mysqldump utility to make ad hoc backups.

- Ask your server administrator to start your MySQL server with the --safe-updates option. Alternatively, you can set this option yourself (but only temporarily) by running the following query: SET SQL_SAFE_UPDATES=1; Amusingly, a synonym for this option is --i-am-a-dummy.

This option prevents DELETE and UPDATE queries that do not contain a LIMIT or WHERE clause from being run. The danger of DELETE and UPDATE queries without LIMIT or WHERE clauses is that these kinds of queries are applied to the entire table. For example, DELETE FROM foo; deletes every row in table foo.

- If working on a table managed by MyISAM or another non-transactional storage engine, test your queries on a copy of the table before running them on the real table. For example, you could use this set of commands to copy a table:

```
CREATE TEMPORARY TABLE test LIKE book;
INSERT test SELECT * FROM book;
```

Then run your commands on the test table, double-check that they work as anticipated, and then run them on table book.

This approach only works with a moderate-sized database. If you have hundreds of thousands or millions of rows of data, it might take too much of your server's resources to test in this fashion.

- If you are using tables managed by a transactional storage engine such as InnoDB or BerkeleyDB, see the following phrase for instructions on how to safely test queries inside of a transaction.

If you do accidentally destroy valuable data, see Chapter 10.

MANIPULATING DATA

Testing Queries Inside of a Transaction

If you are working on a table managed by a transactional storage engine, such as InnoDB or BDB, you can safely test many types of queries within the context of a transaction. If the queries operate as you expect, the transaction can be committed and made permanent. If the queries do not work as anticipated, you can roll them back and return the database to the state that it was in before the transaction started.

> **CAUTION**
>
> Not all types of query can be rolled back, including all of the CREATE and DROP queries.

> **TIP**
>
> Ensure that you are working with tables that are managed by a transactional storage engine by using the SHOW CREATE TABLE query. If a table is managed by a transaction storage engine, the ENGINE option of the CREATE TABLE statement generated by SHOW CREATE TABLE should be set to InnoDB or BDB.

Here is an example of testing commands within the context of a transaction:

```
# Ensure you are dealing with a transactional table
# Look for the line ENGINE=InnoDB
SHOW CREATE TABLE book;
```

```
BEGIN; # start your transaction
UPDATE book SET author = "Dr. Seuss";
SELECT * FROM book; # examine results and
# ... notice that data has been overwritten
ROLLBACK; # cancel the transaction

SELECT * FROM book; # See? All the data is safe.

BEGIN; # start a new transaction
UPDATE book SET AUTHOR = "Dr. Seuss"
  WHERE author = "Theodor Geisel";
SELECT * FROM book; # examine results
COMMIT; # make changes permanent
```

An Overview of Updating Column Values

Although data is inserted into a table one or more rows at a time, it can be updated in a variety of ways, ranging from changing a single field (one column in one row) to changing all values in one or more columns across one or more rows.

The updates are accomplished with the UPDATE command. UPDATE allows you to specify new values for one or more columns in one or more tables. In its most basic form, the command specifies a new value for a given column in all rows in a single table.

```
UPDATE book SET cond = 'mint'; # DON'T RUN THIS
```

This query changes the value of cond in every row to be 'mint', which is probably not desired. In a production database, a tiny mental hiccough or a slip of the fingers can trash every value in one or more columns across every row in a table. Usually, a WHERE clause is used to specify under what conditions a column should be updated.

A more typical use of UPDATE would be:

```
UPDATE book
SET author = "Theodor Geisel"
WHERE author = "Dr. Seuss";
```

In this example, the author column is updated in the book table, but only for the rows where column author is equal to "Dr. Seuss".

At this point, let's take a closer look at the syntax of an UPDATE query. The major parts are

- **UPDATE**—Indicates the type of query you are running and is followed by the name of the table on which the query should run.

- **SET**—Marks that you will be specifying a list of the names one or columns to update, along with the values (or expressions) with which the columns should be updated. Each name/value pair is separated by an equal sign (=). Multiple name/value pairs are separated with commas, as in

  ```
  SET name0='value', name1='some_other_value',
  ...
  ```

- **WHERE**—An optional WHERE clause is used to restrict on which rows the UPDATE will operate. For more information, see Chapter 4, "Retrieving Data: Simple Queries."

More complex uses of UPDATE allow you to update multiple columns simultaneously or to update columns with values that are based on formulas. For examples and information, see the following phrases.

Updating Columns with Formulas

```
UPDATE loan
SET date_lent = DATE_ADD(date_lent, INTERVAL 1 YEAR)
WHERE date_lent = '2005-01-01';
```

Assume that in the wee hours of the New Year, you loaned visiting friends five books, recorded the loans in a table called loan, and accidentally entered the wrong year in the date stored in date_lent. The simple UPDATE statement in the phrasebox allows you to correct the issue for all five rows in one query.

The formula used in the previous sample query is simple enough—a new date is calculated by using MySQL's DATE_ADD function to add a week to an existing date. The interesting thing is that the new value assigned to date_lent is based on the existing value of date_lent. The feature of UPDATE that allows the query to reference existing values in the table is part of what makes this type of query so useful.

Deleting Rows

```
DELETE FROM book WHERE cond = 'poor';
```

Assume that you have decided that it is time to permanently retire any books in your library that are in poor condition. The simple DELETE query in the phrasebox accomplishes exactly that.

The basic syntax for DELETE is

```
DELETE FROM table_name WHERE some_conditions;
```

The WHERE clause used in the DELETE command is the same familiar WHERE clause used in SELECT and UPDATE commands. For more information, see Chapter 4.

Deleting Rows from Multiple Tables

```
DELETE book, loan     # tables to delete from
FROM book, loan       # tables to use in WHERE clause
WHERE book.book_id = loan.book_id
AND book.cond = 'poor';
```

A more complex form of the DELETE query allows you to delete rows from multiple tables in one operation. In the phrasebox, you are deleting any books that are in poor condition, along with any loans of those books.

The syntax for this kind of DELETE is as follows:

- **DELETE**—Indicates the start of a DELETE query and should be immediately followed by a list of tables.

- *list, of, tables, ...*—Immediately following the DELETE keyword is a list of one or more tables. Only tables listed here will have rows deleted from them.

- **FROM**—Used to mark which tables should be a part of the WHERE clause of the query.

- *list, of, tables, ...*—Only tables contained in this list may be used in the WHERE clause of the query.

- **WHERE**—A standard WHERE clause. Rows that match conditions in the WHERE clause and that are in tables listed immediately after the DELETE keyword will be deleted. For more information on WHERE clauses, see Chapter 4.

See Also

The following sections of the online reference manual provide more information about the topics covered in this chapter:

- **UPDATE Syntax**—http://dev.mysql.com/doc/refman/5.0/en/update.html

- **DELETE Syntax**—http://dev.mysql.com/doc/refman/5.0/en/delete.html

- **START TRANSACTION, COMMIT, and ROLLBACK Syntax**—http://dev.mysql.com/doc/refman/5.0/en/commit.html

6

User Management and Security

$M_{y}SQL$ is a multi-user database with a sophisticated access control system. The phrases in this chapter will show you how to maintain the users on your database and to give each user only the permissions he requires.

MySQL's privilege system ensures that each user may only perform the operations that he is allowed. A user's identity is determined by a given username and the remote address from which the connection is made. A user is also usually required to authenticate by providing a password when connecting to the database.

TIP

You need specific administrator privileges to perform each of the commands in this chapter. If you connect to MySQL as the root user—typical for performing user maintenance—you have the appropriate permissions to execute every example phrase.

Creating Users

```
CREATE USER user@host IDENTIFIED BY 'password';
```

To create a new user, you must have sufficient administrator rights. Specifically, you must have either the CREATE USER privilege or INSERT privilege on the mysql database. These permissions are covered in the "Tailoring User Permissions" phrase later in this chapter.

The following example creates a new user named zak who can only connect to MySQL from the IP address 123.456.78.90 and the password given. A login attempt using username zak from any other host will be rejected, regardless of whether the password supplied is correct.

```
CREATE USER 'zak'@'123.456.78.90'
IDENTIFIED BY 'phrasebook';
```

The host specifier can be an IP address, a local hostname, or a fully qualified domain name. To create a user that can connect to a MySQL database running on the local machine, use localhost:

```
CREATE USER 'zak'@'localhost'
IDENTIFIED BY 'localuser';
```

NOTE

For web scripts using a MySQL database that runs on the same machine as the web server, you always open a connection to localhost in the script.

> **TIP**
> Typically you allow database access from a web script using a single MySQL username and password, even if your application performs additional user authentication.

The previous two examples can both be executed on the same MySQL database, and the result is that two separate users are created. Although both are named zak, one can only log in from the remote host and only using the password phrasebook, whereas the second can log in only from the local machine, with the password localuser.

The CREATE USER command was added in MySQL version 5.0.2. In earlier versions, users could be created automatically when assigning permissions using the GRANT command (discussed in the "Tailoring User Permissions" phrase later in this chapter) or by manually inserting records into the mysql database.

The mysql database contains three tables—user, host, and db—which contain the database permissions.

The user table contains the usernames and passwords of everyone who has access to any part of the MySQL database. The values of Host and User together specify the remote user, and Password contains an encrypted password string.

As an administrator, you can insert records directly into these tables, but must use the PASSWORD() function to generate the correctly encrypted password string. The following example is equivalent to the previous CREATE USER example:

```
INSERT INTO user (Host, User, Password)
VALUES ('123.456.78.90', 'zak',
         PASSWORD('phrasebook'));

FLUSH PRIVILEGES;
```

The FLUSH PRIVILEGES command is required to tell
MySQL to reload the privilege data after you make a
change. This is not required with the CREATE USER
command.

Deleting Users

DROP USER *user@host*;

The DROP USER command removes records from the
mysql.user table, effectively deleting that user account.
Deleting a user does not immediately terminate an
active user session, but it does prevent all future connections from being authorized for that username.

The DROP USER command was added in MySQL 5.0.2.
In earlier versions of MySQL, you must revoke the
user's privileges first, delete the records from user manually, and then issue the FLUSH PRIVILEGES command.

```
DELETE FROM user
WHERE User = 'zak'
AND Host = '123.456.78.90';

FLUSH PRIVILEGES;
```

Renaming a User

```
RENAME USER old_user@host TO new_user@host;
```

You rename a MySQL user only very occasionally, but sometimes you need to—for instance, if your usernames are based on a user's real name and the person gets married. If Denise Black changes her surname to White, you would execute the following command to update her username:

```
RENAME USER dblack@localhost TO dwhite@locahost;
```

The RENAME USER command has been available since MySQL 5.0.2. In earlier versions of MySQL, you have to update the user table by hand, along with any corresponding rows in db, remembering to use the FLUSH PRIVIGES command afterward:

```
UPDATE user
SET User = 'dwhite'
WHERE User = 'dblack'
AND Host = 'localhost';

UPDATE db
SET User = 'dwhite'
WHERE User = 'dblack'
AND Host = 'localhost';

FLUSH PRIVILEGES;
```

Using Wildcards

The SQL wildcard characters, % and _, can be used in the privilege system to denote that access is granted when the connection parameters match the given pattern. Most commonly, you want to allow access from a range of hosts without having to create multiple user accounts for the same person. The following statement creates a user zak that can connect from any host on the 192.168.0.x IP range.

```
CREATE USER 'zak'@'192.168.0.%'
IDENTIFIED BY 'phrasebook';
```

If you are happy to rely on username/password authentication only and want to allow logins for a user from any host, simply use % for the hostname:

```
CREATE USER 'zak'@'%' IDENTIFIED BY 'phrasebook';
```

Finding Users of a Given Database or Table

```
SELECT Db FROM db
WHERE User = 'user' AND Host = 'host';

SELECT Table_name FROM tables_priv
WHERE User = 'user'
AND Host = 'host' AND Db = 'db';
```

To find out which users have access to a given database, query the db table using the User and Host columns. The Db column contains the database name.

To find out specific tables to which a user has access, query the tables_priv table. The phrase shown in the phrasebox assumes you will supply the User, Host, and Db values. Alternatively, the following example finds the database and table names to which a user has access:

```
SELECT Db, Table_name FROM tables_priv
WHERE User = 'zak' AND Host = 'localhost';
```

To find the specific privileges that a user has, use the SHOW GRANTS command, discussed in the "Viewing a User's Privileges" phrase later in this chapter.

Setting Passwords

```
SET PASSWORD = PASSWORD('password');

SET PASSWORD FOR user@host = PASSWORD('password');
```

When you are connected to MySQL as a regular user, use the first syntax to change your own password. If you connected as an administrator, you can change the password for another user as follows:

```
SET PASSWORD FOR zak@localhost =
    PASSWORD('flibble');
```

In fact to change another user's password you must have the UPDATE privilege on the mysql.user table. The SET PASSWORD command is available in all versions of MySQL, but you can also modify passwords by changing values in the user table. The previous command is equivalent to the following UPDATE statement:

```
UPDATE user
SET Password = PASSWORD('flibble')
WHERE User = 'zak' AND Host = 'localhost';
```

Remember, you must issue a FLUSH PRIVILEGES command after making any changes to the user table. This is not required if you use the SET PASSWORD command.

Tailoring User Permissions

```
GRANT privileges ON db.table
TO user@host
IDENTIFIED BY 'password';
```

Use the GRANT command to give a database user a set of privileges on a database or on a list of tables. The GRANT command creates the specified user account if it does not already exist. In fact, in MySQL version 4.1 and earlier where there is no CREATE USER command, you have to use GRANT to create a new user.

The privileges that can be set are shown in Table 6.1. Specifying ALL PRIVILEGES grants each of these options.

Table 6.1   **Privileges Allocated Using** GRANT

Privilege	Meaning
ALTER	Allows use of ALTER TABLE.
ALTER ROUTINE	Alter or drop stored routines.
CREATE	Allows use of CREATE TABLE.
CREATE ROUTINE	Create stored routines.
CREATE TEMPORARY TABLES	Allows use of CREATE TEMPORARY TABLE.
CREATE USER	Allows use of CREATE USER, DROP USER, RENAME USER, and REVOKE ALL PRIVILEGES.
CREATE VIEW	Allows use of CREATE VIEW.
DELETE	Allows use of DELETE.
DROP	Allows use of DROP TABLE.

Table 6.1 **Continued**

Privilege	Meaning
EXECUTE	Allows the user to run stored routines.
FILE	Allows use of SELECT ... INTO OUTFILE and LOAD DATA INFILE.
INDEX	Allows use of CREATE INDEX and DROP INDEX.
INSERT	Allows use of INSERT.
LOCK TABLES	Allows use of LOCK TABLES on tables for which you also have SELECT privileges.
PROCESS	Allows use of SHOW FULL PROCESSLIST.
RELOAD	Allows use of FLUSH.
REPLICATION CLIENT	Allows the user to ask where slave or master servers are.
REPLICATION SLAVE	Needed for replication slaves.
SELECT	Allows use of SELECT.
SHOW DATABASES	Allows use of SHOW DATABASES.
SHOW VIEW	Allows use of SHOW CREATE VIEW.
SHUTDOWN	Allows use of mysqladmin shutdown.

USER MANAGEMENT AND SECURITY

Table 6.1 **Continued**

Privilege	Meaning
SUPER	Allows use of CHANGE MASTER, KILL, PURGE MASTER LOGS, and SET GLOBAL SQL statements. Allows mysqladmin debug command. Allows one extra connection to be made if maximum connections are reached.
UPDATE	Allows use of UPDATE.
USAGE	Allows connection without any specific privileges.

A comma-separated list of privileges can be used with GRANT to give a user several permissions in one statement. The following example gives the user zak permission to query the table mytable and insert new records, but not to update or delete existing records:

```
GRANT SELECT, INSERT ON sampdb.mytable
TO 'zak'@'localhost' IDENTIFIED BY 'phrasebook';
```

To give a user all the privileges listed in Table 6.1, you can use ALL PRIVILEGES, or simply the keyword ALL, in the GRANT statement. The following example gives zak full access to the table:

```
GRANT ALL PRIVILEGES ON sampdb.mytable
TO 'zak'@'localhost' IDENTIFIED BY 'phrasebook';
```

If you are granting new privileges to a user that already exists, you do not need to specify the IDENTIFIED BY clause. If IDENTIFIED BY is used, the user's password is overwritten. If it is omitted, the password remains unchanged.

Allowing Other Users to Grant Privileges

```
GRANT privileges ON db.table
TO user@host
IDENTIFIED BY 'password'
WITH GRANT OPTION;
```

Even granting ALL PRIVILEGES to a user does not enable that user to pass on those rights to another user on the system. In fact, it is rare that the database administrator would want to give that kind of access to another user, so a special instruction is needed in the GRANT statement.

By suffixing the GRANT command with WITH GRANT OPTION, you enable a user to use the privileges specified, and to reassign them to another user.

You should take care when using WITH GRANT OPTION. Although a user cannot grant another user a privilege he does not have, two users with different permissions could effectively combine their privileges!

Viewing a User's Privileges

```
SHOW GRANTS;
SHOW GRANTS FOR user;
```

The SHOW GRANTS command can be used to ascertain what privileges a user has. The output is a list of GRANT statements that can be used to reproduce the same permissions if you had to assign them to the user again.

```
SHOW GRANTS FOR 'zak'@'localhost';
```

The result might look something like this:

```
+-------------------------------------------------+
| Grants for zak@localhost                        |
+-------------------------------------------------+
| GRANT USAGE ON zakdb.* TO 'zak'@'localhost'     |
| IDENTIFIED BY PASSWORD '57104f8717923cb5'       |
| GRANT SELECT, INSERT ON `sampdb`.`mytable`      |
| TO 'zak'@'localhost'                            |
+-------------------------------------------------+
```

Notice that this output indicates that a password has been set, but only an encrypted password is shown. You cannot decode this string back to the user's actual password.

Issuing SHOW GRANTS with no FOR clause shows the privileges for the current user. It is equivalent to

```
SHOW GRANTS FOR CURRENT_USER();
```

Removing User Access

```
REVOKE privileges ON db.table
FROM user@host;
```

Use REVOKE to remove one or more privileges from a user. Use a comma-separated list of privileges or ALL PRIVILEGES to remove all the permissions shown in Table 6.1. To remove all access for a user, including the GRANT OPTION, use a statement like this:

```
REVOKE ALL PRIVILEGES, GRANT OPTION
ON sampdb.mytable
FROM 'zak'@'localhost';
```

Disabling Network Access

`skip-networking`

To disable remote access via TCP/IP, add
`skip-networking` to `my.cnf`, or start `mysqld` using the
`--skip-networking` switch. MySQL will then only
accept connections from the local host via a socket.

If network access is disabled, users are not able to connect to MySQL from remote hosts even if they have a
user account that would otherwise allow them to do so.

If you do allow remote access to MySQL, any firewall
that sits between your MySQL server and the outside
world must allow traffic on the appropriate port. By
default, this is port 3306.

Disabling User Authentication

`skip-grant-tables`

Suppose that somehow you have lost the password for
your superuser login and need to reset the password.
To set a new password, you need to tell MySQL to
restart with user authentication disabled.

To do this, you have to have system administration
rights to be able to shut down and restart the `mysqld`
process. After stopping the MySQL server, add
`skip-grant-tables` to your master `my.cnf` file.
Alternatively, start `mysqld` with the `--skip-grant-tables`
switch.

With MySQL started in this mode, you can connect
without a password using simply

```
mysql -u root
```

Then you can set a new password for root in the usual way. To begin authenticating users, issue the FLUSH PRIVILEGES statement or restart the MySQL server without skip-grant-tables.

CAUTION

Be aware that while mysqld is running with skip-grant-tables, any user may connect without needing to be authenticated. Therefore, if you ever do need to perform this step, do it as quickly as possible! You can also protect yourself by blocking network access using skip-networking and ensuring that no users are logged into the local machine in order to connect to localhost.

Using SSL-Secured Connection

MySQL can use SSL to encrypt network connections between the database server and a client. This facility must be enabled in your server at compile time, and to check whether it is available run the following command:

```
SHOW VARIABLES LIKE 'have_openssl';
```

The result either shows Yes or No alongside this variable, indicating whether the facility is available. If it is not, you must recompile your MySQL server using the --with-vio and --with-openssl configure switches.

NOTE

Since MySQL 5.0.10, MySQL has built-in support for SSL-encrypted network connections, using yaSSL. To activate this at compile time, use --with-yassl=yes. Usage is otherwise the same as the OpenSSL version.

To establish an encrypted SSL connection, you must already have three certificate files, or be able to generate them: a Certificate Authority (CA) certificate, a server certificate, and a client certificate.

Add the following lines to the [mysqld] section of the my.cnf to specify the locations of each of the SSL certificate files that are to be used for a connection to your server:

```
ssl-ca=/path/to/CA-cert
ssl-cert=/path/to/server-cert
ssl-key=/path/to/client-cert
```

The client settings can be added to the [client] section of my.cnf, and are identical to the server settings. You must use the same three certificate files for the client as for the server.

Alternatively, you can specify each certificate as a command-line argument to mysql:

```
mysql --ssl-ca=/path/to/CA-cert \
    --ssl-cert=/path/to/server-cert \
    --ssl-key=/path/to/client-cert
```

See Also

The following sections of the online reference manual provide more information about the topics covered in this chapter:

- **Account Management Statements**—http://dev.mysql.com/doc/refman/5.0/en/account-management-sql.html

- **FLUSH Syntax**—http://dev.mysql.com/doc/refman/5.0/en/flush.html

USER MANAGEMENT AND SECURITY

- **The MySQL Access Privilege System**—
  http://dev.mysql.com/doc/refman/5.0/en/
  privilege-system.html

- **Security-Related mysqld Options**—http://
  dev.mysql.com/doc/refman/5.0/en/
  privileges-options.html

- **Using Secure Connections**—http://
  dev.mysql.com/doc/refman/5.0/en/
  secure-connections.html

7

The mysql Command-line Client

Many interactive clients are available for MySQL. The clients range in type from familiar desktop applications that have a graphical user interface (GUI) to web-based applications accessed via an Internet browser to text-only applications that run from a shell.

This chapter focuses on mysql, the interactive text-only command-line client that comes with the MySQL server. Although other tools might be slightly friendlier to novices, learning how to use the mysql tool teaches you the fundamentals required to use any other kind of tool. Additionally, mysql might be the only tool you have for interacting with a given MySQL server, and it is best that you know enough about it to be productive.

Connecting to a MySQL Server

```
shell> mysql [-h host] [-u user_name] [-p] [db_name]
```

Connections to a local MySQL server with the `mysql` command-line client are easy to make. Simply run `mysql`, providing these optional arguments:

- **-h**—Specify the host to which you want to connect. If you omit the -h option, `mysql` attempts to connect to a server on the local machine.

- **-u**—Specify the user you want to connect as. If you do not specify a -u option, `mysql` uses your Unix username to attempt to authenticate to MySQL.

- **-p**—Tell `mysql` to prompt you for a password. You can create accounts without passwords or specify the password to use as an argument on the command line. Neither approach is recommended because both significantly compromise the security of your MySQL accounts and installations.

- **database_name**—The name of the database on which you want to operate. If you don't specify this on connection or want to change it later, use the USE command, as in USE `database_name;`.

Other arguments can be specified to change how `mysql` behaves or to where it attempts to connect. Run `mysql -?` to see a complete list of possible arguments.

If you are unfamiliar with user accounts, see Chapter 6, "User Management and Security," for more information.

Using the Client in Batch Mode

```
shell> echo 'SELECT 1 + 1' | mysql -u some_user -p
```

mysql can also be used in batch mode, allowing queries to be passed in from standard input and the results to be sent to standard output. The phrasebox example shows how to send a simple query to mysql via stdin and display the result of the query.

Like most other shell commands, mysql can be combined with other commands using pipes and input redirection. For example, the following shell command reads commands from file input_file and passes them to mysql. In turn, mysql authenticates the user, and if authentication succeeds, processes the commands and returns the results. The results are written to a file called output_file.

```
shell> mysql -u user -p < input_file > output_file
```

For more information on the pipe and input redirection features of your favorite shell, see the documentation for the shell.

Basic mysql Command-line Client Navigation

On Unix-like operating systems, such as Linux and Mac OS X, mysql includes the GNU Readline library—a powerful tool that allows you to quickly navigate around the command line. Readline includes more than 100 commands, but only the dozen or so most useful commands are covered here. If you want to learn more about Readline, run man readline from your shell.

Some of the most useful key bindings (along with handy mnemonics to help you remember them) are

- **Go to line start**—CTRL+a. Remember that *a* is the first letter of the alphabet.

- **Go to line end**—CTRL+e. Remember that *e* stands for end.

- **Move one word backward**—ALT+b. Remember that *b* stands for backward.

- **Move one word forward**—ALT+f. Remember that *f* stands for forward.

- **Delete previous word**—CTRL+w. Remember that *w* stands for word.

- **Delete to start of line**—CTRL+u.

- **Clear screen**—CTRL+l (lowercase L).

- **Uppercase/lowercase previous word**—ALT+u or ALT+l (lowercase L). Remember ALTer to uppercase or lowercase.

- **Undo previous typing**—ALT+_.

> **TIP**
>
> Mac OS X Terminal.app users: You need to change the behavior of your option key in order to use the alt key bindings (such as ALT+f). Follow these steps:
>
> 1. Open `Terminal.app`.
> 2. Select the Terminal menu.
> 3. Select the Window Settings submenu.
> 4. A dialog window named Terminal Inspector opens.
> 5. Select the Keyboard option from the select list at the top of the Terminal Inspector dialog window.
> 6. Ensure that the Use Option Key as Meta Key check box is checked.

Erasing the Current Line or Query

```
mysql> DROP DATABASE foo;\c
```

Most users of command-line shells like Bash are accustomed to using CTRL+c to halt a command or clear a line. Within the `mysql` command-line client, CTRL+c causes the entire program to exit. Instead of CTRL+c, type `\c` and press Enter. This clears the current command and returns you to an empty command-line.

Setting Connection Defaults with an Option File

Repeatedly entering connection details every time you start `mysql` can become tedious. An alternative is to specify options for `mysql` to use in a file.

You can still override these options on the command line when you run mysql. The options in the file (usually) just provide you with a way to specify safer and more convenient behavior.

To specify options that apply to all instances of mysql run on a given system, modify my.cnf (the global MySQL configuration file). To specify options for a specific user on a Unix-like operating system, create a file called .my.cnf in the user's home directory.

Regardless of which file is used, the method for setting the options in the file is the same. First, set a heading of the form [client] on a line by itself. Any options set after this heading, until another heading or the end of the file, are options set for mysql when it starts.

The options that may be set after the [client] header are the same as the available command line options for mysql, with a few small and important differences:

- Leading dashes are omitted. Instead of writing --host, write host.

- The long form of the options should be used. Use host instead of h.

- Place an equal sign between the option name and the option value. host=localhost.

- Comments can be indicated with a leading #.

You might want to set these global options:

```
[client]
# protection from sending unintended queries
disable-reconnect

# save novices from themselves
safe-updates
```

```
# increase safety by showing user
# and host in prompt
prompt='\u@\h> '

# force password prompt
password
```

If you are setting options for a Unix user, you might want to set the most commonly used connection details, including user, host, socket (if needed), and so on.

```
[client]
user=some_user
host=example.com
# don't use compress for talking to a local server
compress        # enable client-server compression
```

> **TIP**
> Options are first read from the global MySQL configuration file, then from the per-user configuration file, and then from the command line.

For more information on what options can be set, run `mysql -?`.

Getting Help Within mysql

If you are working within the mysql command-line client and want to quickly look up a particular command or function, just type **help *command_or_ function_name*** and press Enter. In modern versions of MySQL, concise information on the command or function name is displayed. To see a list of what help is available, type help contents.

This feature is particularly useful when you are visiting a MySQL server that uses an unfamiliar version of MySQL because it often allows you to get help specific to that version of MySQL.

Editing Complex Commands with a Text Editor

Although the mysql environment is convenient for entering small queries, it can be very tedious to enter long queries. If you find that a query is getting overly long or needs serious editing, type \e at the end of the query and press Enter. This feature is not available on Windows systems.

The editor referred to by the $EDITOR environment variable opens, with the query to be edited already in place. Edit the query as you would any other text, save the file (which will have an odd-looking name), and exit the editor.

The query is loaded into mysql, but is not executed. To execute the query, type ; (or \G to display the query results in a list instead of in a table), and press Enter.

See your shell documents for information on how to set the $EDITOR environment variable.

> **TIP**
>
> The default editor might be vi or vim. Although these are both fine editors, they can be very challenging to use for those unfamiliar with them. If you want to bravely forge ahead, type :help<enter> to get help on using the editor. If you want to sensibly retreat, type :q!<enter>.

Database, Table, and Column Name Completion

When writing queries, you can save yourself time by entering the first few characters of a database, table, or column name, and then pressing the Tab key. mysql examines a list of database, table, and column names that it built dynamically when starting (or when switching to another default database via USE) and tries to complete the name for you.

If you have created a new table or otherwise modified the data on the server, type \# and press Enter to rebuild the list of names.

Using the Command-line History

Another exceedingly useful feature of the mysql command-line client is that all of the commands executed for a given session are kept in a buffer for examination and reuse.

If you want to revisit commands you have run, press the up arrow (or CTRL+p). To scroll back down through the entries, press the down arrow (or CTRL+n). If you want to rerun a query you are examining, press Enter. Alternatively, you can edit the query (just as you would any query you had typed in), and then rerun it.

If you want to search through the command history, press CTRL+r and then begin typing in part of a previous command. The last command, if any, that matches what you have typed is displayed. To find the previous matching entry, press CTRL+r again.

To return to the end of the history buffer, press ALT+>. Similarly, to see the first entry in the history buffer, press ALT+<.

Other Useful Tools

Another set of tools that deserves attention is the MySQL Administrator and MySQL Query Browser. Both are open-source cross-platform (Linux, Mac OS X, and Windows) GUI applications that are distributed free of charge by MySQL AB. The MySQL Query Browser provides an excellent environment for making and refining ad-hoc queries, while the MySQL Administrator provides a digital dashboard for one or more MySQL servers that can greatly increase the productivity of both novice and experienced MySQL administrators. Visit http://mysql.com/downloads to get your copies.

MySQL APIs

With a number of APIs, you can use a MySQL database in applications written in various programming languages. Even if no specific language API exists, you can still use Open Database Connectivity (ODBC) to communicate with a MySQL server.

In this chapter you will find brief examples of how to connect to a database, perform a query, and retrieve the results using the most popular APIs.

The C Language API

The C API is the underlying interface used by all the other APIs, and almost every function call in another language's API maps directly to a corresponding C library function.

To use the C API you must link your program with the libmysqlclient.so library that is installed automatically if you compile MySQL from source. For those binary distributions that are split into separate components, you need to install the Libraries and Header Files package for your platform, named MySQL-devel-*.

A C program using the MySQL API must include the mysql.h file that resides in your system's default include directory. You would use the following:

```
#include <mysql/mysql.h>
```

Linking to libmysqlclient.so depends on your compiler, but the following example shows a basic example of how you would compile a mytest.c using the MySQL API using gcc:

```
shell> gcc -o mytest mytest.c -lmysqlclient
```

If you encounter error messages when compiling, you can use the mysql_config utility to find out what compiler options are required. The --cflags, --include, and --libs switches cause mysql_config to display the compiler flags and defines and to include path and library options, respectively.

```
shell> mysql_config  --cflags --include --libs
-I/usr/include/mysql -mcpu=i486
➥ -fno-strength-reduce
-I/usr/include/mysql
-L/usr/lib/mysql -lmysqlclient -lcrypt
➥ -lnsl -lm -lz -lc -lnss_files
➥ -lnss_dns -lresolv -lc -lnss_files -lnss_dns
➥ -lresolv
```

Connecting to MySQL

```
MYSQL mysql;
mysql_init(&mysql);
mysql_real_connect(&mysql, "host", "user",
                   "password", "dbname",
                   port, unix_socket, client_flag);
```

Two function calls are required to connect to a MySQL database. First, you must initialize a MYSQL type object and then use this object as an argument to the mysql_real_connect() function. That object is then used as a resource argument to subsequent API calls to indicate which database connection to use.

The *port* argument is the TCP/IP port used to connect to the database. For localhost connections, this value should be zero. The *unix_socket* argument is NULL unless you want to specify a different socket or named pipe to use for the connection.

The *client_flag* argument should remain NULL unless you need to enable certain features of the MySQL client library, which are not covered in this chapter.

The return value from mysql_real_connect() is a MYSQL object if the connection is successful. The value is the same as the object passed in the first argument, so you do not need to assign this new object to a variable. The function returns NULL if the connection fails for any reason.

Executing a Query

```
mysql_query(&mysql, "query");
mysql_real_query(&mysql, "query", length);
```

The query argument passed to mysql_query() should be a null-terminated string containing a single SQL query. The terminating semicolon is not required. This query is executed against the database connection defined in the MYSQL object passed in the first argument.

If your query contains binary data, you must use mysql_real_query() and specify the length of the query string. Binary data may contain the \0 character, which mysql_query() treats as the end of the string.

The return value is NULL on success, or one of the values shown in Table 8.1 if there is an error.

Table 8.1 Error Codes from mysql_query()

Value	Meaning
CR_COMMANDS_OUT_OF_SYNC	Commands were executed in an improper order.
CR_SERVER_GONE_ERROR	The MySQL server has gone away.
CR_SERVER_LOST	The connection to the server was lost during the query.
CR_UNKNOWN_ERROR	An unknown error occurred.

Fetching Data from a Result Set

```
MYSQL_RES result;
MYSQL_ROW row;
result = mysql_use_result(&mysql);
row = mysql_fetch_row(result);
```

Before you can fetch the data returned by a query in your application, you have to assign the result of that query to a MYSQL_RES object. The mysql_use_result() function assigns the result to this type of object using the most recently executed query on the specified database connection.

After assigning the result, you can continue to execute further queries without destroying the reference to this query result. mysql_use_result() returns NULL on success or the error codes from Table 8.1 on failure.

The mysql_fetch_row() function fetches data from the query one row at a time and returns each row into a MYSQL_ROW structure. Values are then accessed as row[0] up to row[n-1], where n is the number of columns in the data set.

To loop through the entire data set, use mysql_num_fields(result) and mysql_num_rows(result) to find the number of columns and rows returned, respectively. You can also use a while loop to fetch each row in turn, as mysql_fetch_row() returns NULL when there are no more rows to be fetched. The example program in Listing 8.1 later in this chapter shows this in action.

> **NOTE**
>
> You can use mysql_query() to execute any SQL statement—it does not have to be a SELECT query. It is nonsense, however, to try retrieving data rows from an INSERT, UPDATE, or DELETE operation, and doing so causes an error.

Displaying Error Messages

```
mysql_errno(&mysql);
mysql_error(&mysql);
```

Whenever MySQL encounters an error, you can find the internal error number and the corresponding error message using the `mysql_errno()` and `mysql_error()` functions.

Their arguments are the MYSQL connection object, and the error information returned relates to the last query executed on this connection. If the most recent query was successful, `mysql_errno()` returns 0 and `mysql_error()` returns NULL.

You can use these functions to find the cause of an error both when connecting to a database and when executing a query.

Closing a Connection

```
mysql_close(&mysql);
```

When you are done with a MySQL connection, you should close it using `mysql_close()`. The resources allocated by `mysql_init()` are de-allocated.

A Sample C Program

Listing 8.1 is a sample program that establishes a database connection, executes a query against the sample database, and outputs the result in a tabular format.

Listing 8.1   Executing a Query Using the C API

```
#include <stdio.h>
#include <mysql/mysql.h>

main() {

MYSQL mysql;
MYSQL_RES *result;
```

Listing 8.1 **Continued**

```c
MYSQL_ROW row;
int numrows, numcols, c;

mysql_init(&mysql);

/* Establish a database connection */

if (!mysql_real_connect(&mysql, "localhost",
                        "username", "password",
                        "dbname", 0, NULL, 0))
{
  fprintf(stderr,
    "Failed to connect to database: Error %d:
    %s\n", mysql_errno(&mysql),
    mysql_error(&mysql));
}

/* Execute a query */

char query[] = "SELECT book_id, cond, title
                FROM book";

if (mysql_query(&mysql, query))
{
  fprintf(stderr,
    "Error executing query: Error %d: %s\n",
      mysql_errno(&mysql), mysql_error(&mysql));
}

/* Assign the result handle */

result = mysql_use_result(&mysql);

if (!result)
{
  fprintf(stderr,
```

Listing 8.1 **Continued**

```
      "Error executing query: Error %d: %s\n",
      mysql_errno(&mysql), mysql_error(&mysql));
}

/* Find the number of columns in the result */

numcols = mysql_num_fields(result);

/* Loop through the result set to display it */

while (row = mysql_fetch_row(result)) {
  for(c=0; c<numcols; c++) {
    printf("%s\t", row[c]);
  }
  printf("\n");
}

}
```

The output from running the compiled program looks like the following:

```
1       good    Jacob Two-Two Meets the Hooded Fang
2       mint    In the Night Kitchen
3       poor    How to Be a Grouch
4       good    Green Eggs and Ham
5       (null)  Inferno
```

The Perl API

MySQL connectivity in Perl is performed using the Database Interface (DBI) and a Database Driver (DBD). Perl version 5.6.0 or later is required.

If you do not already have DBI installed, use cpan to download and install it:

```
shell> cpan
cpan> install DBI
```

On Windows platforms using the ActivePerl distribution, use the ppm.bat script to install Perl modules:

```
C:\perl\bin> ppm.bat
ppm> install DBI
```

To add the MySQL database driver, install the DBD::mysql module in the same way.

```
cpan> install DBD::mysql
```

Perl scripts that use the MySQL DBD include the following line (note the unusual capitalization of Mysql that is used in the Perl API):

```
use Mysql;
```

Connecting to MySQL

```
$dbh = Mysql->connect(host, dbname,
                      user, password);
```

The connect method is performed on the Mysql object and a database handle is returned. For localhost connections, use undef as the first argument. A single DBI method calls both mysql_init() and mysql_real_connect() in the underlying C API.

Executing a Query

```
$sth = $dbh->query(query);
```

To execute a query, call the query() method on a data-base handle with the SQL statement as its argument. A statement handle is returned.

Fetching Data from a Result Set

```
@row = $sth->fetchrow;
```

When the fetchrow method is called on a statement handle, a row of data from the result of a query is returned as an array. The first time fetchrow is invoked, the first row from the data set is returned, with subsequent calls returning each row in turn. When no more data is available, the method returns NULL.

The numrows and numfields methods return the number of rows and columns returned for a statement handle.

Displaying Error Messages

```
$errno = $dbh->errno;
$errstr = $dbh->errstr;
```

When the errno and errstr methods can be called on a database handle, they return the error number and error message of the most recent query executed using that connection.

To find connection errors, use the same methods on the Mysql object:

```
$errno = Mysql->errno;
$errstr = Mysql->errstr;
```

Closing a Connection

There is no specific DBI method to close a database connection. Resources are de-allocated automatically when the program exits, but if you want to free resources before the end of a problem, you can simply use the undef command on the handle.

A Sample Perl Script

Listing 8.2 is a sample program that establishes a database connection, executes a query against the sample database, and outputs the result in a tabular format.

Listing 8.2 Executing a Query Using Perl DBI

```perl
#!/usr/bin/perl

use Mysql;

/* Establish a database connection */

$dbh = Mysql->connect(undef, "dbname",
                      "username", "password")
   or die ("Failed to connect to database: Error "
                                 . Mysql->errstr);

/* Execute a query */

$sql_statement = "SELECT book_id, cond, title
                  FROM book";
$sth = $dbh->query($sql_statement)
  or die ("Error executing query: Error " .
                             $dbh->errno);

/* Loop through the result set to display it */
```

Listing 8.2   **Continued**

```perl
while (@row = $sth->fetchrow) {
  for($i=0; $i<$sth->numfields; $i++) {
    print $row[$i] . "\t";
  }
  print "\n";
}
```

The output of this script looks just like the output from Listing 8.1.

The PHP API

PHP and MySQL are often spoken in the same breath—a very large number of PHP applications use a MySQL database. For a while PHP even shipped with its own version of the MySQL client library, although this is no longer the case with PHP 5.

To check for MySQL support in a PHP-enabled web server, create a script that simply contains

```php
<?php phpinfo();?>
```

View this script in a web browser and look for a section named either MySQL Support or MySQLi Support. MySQLi (MySQL Improved) is a newer version of the PHP API that works with MySQL 4.1.3 and above and can be used either procedurally or in an object-oriented way. This section covers MySQLi, but the classic MySQL API is very similar to the procedural use of MySQLi.

To enable MySQLi support at compile time, use the `--with-mysql=`/*path/to*/`mysql_config` switch.

Connecting to MySQL

```
$conn = mysqli_connect("host", "user",
                       "password", "dbname");

$conn = new mysqli("host",
                   "user", "password","dbname");
```

The first syntax shown uses the mysqli_connect() function to return a database connection handle using the given arguments. The second form uses the constructor method on a mysqli object to perform the same task.

You must either use the procedural or object-oriented approach throughout your script. Subsequent database operations are either functions that pass the result from mysqli_connect() as an argument or are methods called on a new instance of a mysqli object.

Executing a Query

```
$result = mysqli_query(query, $conn);

$result = $conn->query(query);
```

The query passed in the first argument to mysqli_query() or the query() method both return a result handle. Using the procedural approach, the result handle is passed as an argument to subsequent functions that process the returned data. Using objects, the result itself is an object and you invoke its methods to process the queried data.

Fetching Data from a Result Set

```
$row = mysqli_fetch_array($result);

$result->fetch_array();
```

The mysqli_fetch_array() function returns one data record from the result of a query each time it is called, and the fetch_array() method on a result handle works the same way. When there is no more data to be fetched, both return NULL.

The array returned has both numeric and associative indexes. Numeric index values begin at zero and correspond to the selected columns from left to right. Associative indexes correspond to the column names or aliases in the query.

To find the number of rows returned by the query, reference mysqli_num_rows with a result handle argument or the num_rows attribute on a result object. Use mysqli_num_fields or num_fields to find the number of columns in the data set.

Displaying Error Messages

```
mysqli_error($conn);

$conn->error();
```

The mysqli_error() function takes the connection handle as its argument and returns the MySQL error message if the last query could not be executed. The error() method should be invoked on a database connection object.

To find the MySQL error number, use the
`mysqli_errno()` function and the `error()` method in
the same way.

Closing a Connection

```
mysqli_close($conn);

$conn->close();
```

MySQL resources are automatically destroyed when
your PHP script ends, but if you want to free the
resources in your script, use the `mysqli_close()` function or the `close()` method on a database handle
object.

To free a result resource without closing the database
connection, use `mysqli_free_result()` or the
`free_result()` method on a result object.

A Sample PHP Script

Listing 8.3 is a sample PHP script that establishes a
database connection, executes a query against the sample database, and outputs the result in an HTML table.
This example uses the object-oriented MySQLi API.

Listing 8.3 **Executing a Query Using PHP and MySQLi**

```
<?php

/* Establish a database connection */

$conn = new mysqli("localhost",
                    "user", "password", "dbname");
```

Listing 8.3 **Continued**

```php
if (!$conn) {
  echo "Failed to connect to database: Error " .
                     $conn->error(). "<br>\n";
  exit;
}

/* Execute a query */

$sql_statement = "SELECT book_id, cond, title
                  FROM book";
$result = $conn->query($sql_statement);
if (!$result) {
  echo "Error executing query: Error: " .
                     $conn->error(). "<br>\n";
  exit;
}

/* Loop through the result set to display it */

echo "<table>\n";
while ($row = $result->fetch_array()) {
  echo "<tr>\n";
  for ($i=0; $i<$result->num_rows; $i++) {
    echo "<td>" . $row[$i] . "</td>\n";
  }
  echo "</tr>\n";
}
echo "</table>";

?>
```

This script produces a tabular output like the previous two examples, but this time uses HTML to define the table layout. Run the script in a web browser to see the table.

See Also

The following sections of the online reference manual provide more information about the topics covered in this chapter:

- **C API Function Descriptions**—http://dev.mysql.com/doc/refman/5.0/en/c-api-functions.html

- **MySQL Connector/J (JDBC)**—http://dev.mysql.com/doc/refman/5.0/en/java-connector.html

- **MySQL Connector/NET (.NET)**—http://dev.mysql.com/doc/refman/5.0/en/connector-net.html

- **MySQL Connector/ODBC**—http://dev.mysql.com/doc/refman/5.0/en/odbc-connector.html

- **The MySQL Database Driver for Perl**—http://search.cpan.org/dist/DBD-mysql/lib/Mysql.pm

- **The Perl Database Interface**—http://search.cpan.org/~timb/DBI-1.50/DBI.pm

- **MySQL Improved Extension**—www.php.net/manual/en/ref.mysqli.php

- **MySQL Functions**—www.php.net/manual/en/ref.mysql.php

- **MySQL Python API**—http://dev.mysql.com/doc/refman/5.0/en/python.html

- **MySQL Tcl API**—http://dev.mysql.com/doc/refman/5.0/en/tcl.html

Advanced Queries

In Chapter 4, "Retrieving Data: Simple Queries," you learned how to perform simple database queries using SQL. This chapter deals with more advanced queries, including table joins—one of the most powerful features of SQL.

Joins

Relational databases have the capability to split data across several tables in a structured way so data is never repeated. In general, a column in one table that can uniquely identify a particular row is known as a *primary key* and a column in another table that references that table's primary key is known as a *foreign key*.

Consider the tables in the sample database. The book table has a primary key named book_id, which is a unique numeric value for each book record in the table. Similarly, the primary key on the person table is person_id. The loan table contains details of books loaned to people and references the two other tables. It contains foreign key fields named book_id and person_id that contain numeric values corresponding to rows in their respective tables.

When a book is loaned, therefore, the `loan` table does not have to duplicate any of the information about either the person or the book. The only extra information needed in this table is the date of the loan, stored in the `date_lent` column.

Joining Tables

```
SELECT columns
FROM table1, table2
WHERE table1.foreign_key = table2.primary_key;
```

To combine data from two or more tables to find the detail of records referenced in a foreign key, you have to perform a table join. The most common way to do this is by specifying a list of tables in the FROM clause of a SELECT statement and using the WHERE clause to indicate the relationship between the tables.

The following query returns all the loan data, joining the `loan` table to both `person` and `book`, so that information from those tables can be displayed.

```
SELECT loan.date_lent, person.name, book.title
FROM loan, book, person
WHERE loan.book_id = book.book_id
AND loan.person_id = person.person_id;
```

The prefixes used in this query to indicate which table each column refers to is known as *qualifying* the column. This is essential when the same column name applies to more than one table. If the columns are not properly qualified, MySQL does not make any assumptions about which table a query is referring to and returns an error. It is good practice to always qualify your columns to create clear and easy-to-read queries.

The output from this query looks like the following.

```
+------------+---------+------------------------+
| date_lent  | name    | title                  |
+------------+---------+------------------------+
| 2005-06-05 | Yvette  | Green Eggs and Ham     |
| 2005-07-17 | Thies   | In the Night Kitchen   |
| 2005-07-17 | Thies   | How to Be a Grouch     |
| 2005-09-10 | harmony | Jacob Two-Two Meets    |
|            |         | the Hooded Fang        |
| 2005-10-18 | Thies   | Green Eggs and Ham     |
+------------+---------+------------------------+
```

Additional filters can be applied to a query that contains a join by adding more conditions with the AND keyword.

It is vital to include a WHERE clause when joining tables to indicate the relationship between them. Otherwise, every row from the first table is joined with each row from the second table, creating a data set that is very large and usually not useful!

The JOIN Keyword

```
SELECT columns
FROM table1
JOIN table2
ON table1.foreign_key = table2.primary_key;
```

Another syntax for joins uses the JOIN keyword, with the relationship between two tables given in a separate ON clause. This can make queries more readable because the join conditions are kept separate to any filters in the WHERE clause. It also allows for different types of joins to be performed, such as an outer join.

The following query is identical in behavior to the previous example, using the JOIN syntax:

```
SELECT loan.date_lent, person.name, book.title
FROM loan
JOIN book
ON loan.book_id = book.book_id
JOIN person
ON loan.person_id = person.person_id
```

Table Aliases

In the previous examples, column names were qualified by using the table name as a prefix. Often, and particularly when using a database with longer table names, this can become cumbersome. You might want to use aliases to create a shorter name to refer to the tables in a query.

Use AS to give a table an alias. The AS keyword appears immediately after a table name in the FROM clause or a JOIN clause, as shown in the following example:

```
SELECT l.date_lent, p.name, b.title
FROM loan AS l
JOIN book AS b
ON l.book_id = b.book_id
JOIN person AS p
ON l.person_id = p.person_id
```

The alias is then used as the prefix to qualify a column name, both in the SELECT clause and any conditions in the query. When you use aliases, you must use the alias throughout the query—you cannot also qualify a column using the full table name prefix.

Outer Joins

```
SELECT columns
FROM table1
LEFT OUTER JOIN table2
ON table1.foreign_key = table2.primary_key;
```

The joins in the previous example are known as *inner joins*. A row is only returned by the query if there is data in both tables in the join that meets the join criteria.

Another type of join is an *outer join*, where every row is returned from one table regardless of whether there is a corresponding row in the second table. When this happens, values returned from the second table that do not have corresponding rows in the first table are all given NULL values.

The following query finds the most recent loan date for each person in the database using an outer join:

```
SELECT p.name, MAX(l.date_lent)
FROM person p
LEFT OUTER JOIN loan l
ON p.person_id = l.person_id
GROUP BY p.name;
```

Because one row in the person table does not have any associated loan data, the loan date displayed is NULL. The output is as follows:

```
+---------+-------------------+
| name    | MAX(l.date_lent)  |
+---------+-------------------+
| harmony | 2005-09-10        |
| Lenz    | NULL              |
| Thies   | 2005-10-18        |
| Yvette  | 2005-06-05        |
+---------+-------------------+
```

Column Aliases

Just like you can give a table name an alias using AS, you can give a column an alias. Look back at the output from the previous example, and you will see that the second column's heading contains the function used to generate that value.

By changing the first line of the query to

```
SELECT p.name, MAX(1.date_lent) AS max_date_lent
```

the column heading shows the alias name rather than the column calculation.

When displaying a query using mysql, this is purely a cosmetic issue, but when you develop applications using one of MySQL's APIs, you will usually want to reference the data returned in a computed column using a simple name.

Similarly, suppose you execute a query that returns two columns from different tables but the columns have the same name. You should use a column alias to give each one a unique name so you can identify each one in your application.

Subqueries

MySQL allows you to embed one query within another. The embedded query is known as a *subquery*. Within a SELECT statement, you put another query inside parentheses. The subquery is evaluated first, and its result is used in the main query.

Filtering with a Subquery

```
SELECT columns
FROM table1
WHERE col1 IN (
  SELECT col2
  FROM table2
  WHERE ...
);
```

You can use a subquery in an expression in a WHERE
clause. Usually this is on the right side of the IN operator. The subquery returns a number of rows, and that
result is used as the list of values to compare using IN.
The subquery should return just one column.

The following example uses a subquery to find the
books that are in good or mint condition, and then
uses the result of that query to find the people that
have borrowed those books:

```
SELECT DISTINCT p.name
FROM loan l
JOIN person p
ON p.person_id = l.person_id
WHERE l.book_id IN (
  SELECT book_id FROM book
  WHERE cond in ('mint', 'good')
);
```

Essentially, this query says "show me everyone who has
borrowed a book in good or mint condition." To follow how this is evaluated, take the subquery and execute it separately. If you run

```
SELECT book_id FROM book
WHERE cond IN ('mint', 'good');
```

the result looks like this:

ADVANCED QUERIES

```
+---------+
| book_id |
+---------+
|       1 |
|       2 |
|       4 |
+---------+
```

With this information, you can see that the actual query executed is as follows:

```
SELECT DISTINCT p.name
FROM loan l
JOIN person p
ON p.person_id = l.person_id
WHERE l.book_id IN (1, 2, 4);
```

If you are absolutely sure that a subquery can only ever return one row, you can use it with an equal operator. Be aware, however, that an error occurs if the subquery does return more than one row.

Selecting the Result of a Subquery

```
SELECT columns, (SELECT colums FROM table)
FROM ...
```

You can use a subquery in the SELECT clause, and its result is returned as a column. The subquery must return only one column or MySQL gives an error.

The following example uses two subqueries in the SELECT statement to return two pieces of summary information in a single query. Each subquery performs a COUNT(*) operation on a different table, with the two results ultimately being returned as a single row of data containing two columns.

```
SELECT (SELECT COUNT(*) FROM person) AS num_person,
       (SELECT COUNT(*) FROM book) AS num_book;
```

Correlated Subqueries

If a subquery references a table that also appears in the outer query, it cannot be executed in the way described previously—it is impossible to evaluate the subquery without knowing each row value for the table in the outer query. This is known as a *correlated subquery*.

The following example uses a subquery to return the most recent loan date for each book returned by the main query. This is a correlated subquery because the inner query references the book table from the main query. You cannot execute the subquery on its own without knowing the book.book_id value for each row returned by the main query.

```
SELECT title,
    (SELECT max(date_lent)
     FROM loan
     WHERE loan.book_id = book.book_id) AS subquery
FROM book;
```

As you might have already realized, this query could be rewritten fairly easily using a join and a GROUP BY clause. Frequently, you can perform the same query in several ways, using different joins or subqueries. Sometimes the method used can affect performance— in particular, correlated subqueries can be very slow to execute—so if a query is running slowly, try another method to see if it improves. As correlated subqueries are slow, you should only use one if there is no other way to perform the required query.

Combining Queries with UNION

```
SELECT columns FROM table1
UNION
SELECT columns FROM table2;
```

The UNION keyword is used to join the result of two or more queries together into a single dataset result.

In the following example, the query returns the names of both the authors from the book table and the borrowers from the person table:

```
SELECT author FROM book
UNION
SELECT name FROM person;
```

All tables combined using the UNION operator must return the same number of columns. The column names from the first query are used on the eventual result set—for instance, the previous example returns all the names in a column named author, even though some of the data originated in the person.name column.

By default, only unique rows are returned when you combine queries using UNION. If you want every row to be returned, use UNION ALL.

The following example performs two queries on book. The first query finds the names of books in mint condition. The second finds books where the author's name begins with the letter *M*.

```
SELECT title FROM book
WHERE cond = 'mint'
UNION ALL
SELECT title FROM book
WHERE author LIKE 'M%';
```

The output is as follows. Using UNION ALL causes *In the Night Kitchen* to be displayed twice, as it meets both criteria. The same query using UNION would only return this book once.

```
+------------------------------------+
| title                              |
+------------------------------------+
| In the Night Kitchen               |
| Jacob Two-Two Meets the Hooded Fang |
| In the Night Kitchen               |
+------------------------------------+
```

See Also

The following sections of the online reference manual provide more information about the topics covered in this chapter:

- **JOIN Syntax**—http://dev.mysql.com/doc/refman/5.0/en/join.html

- **Subquery Syntax**—http://dev.mysql.com/doc/refman/5.0/en/subqueries.html

- **UNION Syntax**—http://dev.mysql.com/doc/refman/5.0/en/union.html

Troubleshooting and Emergencies

After you have a running MySQL database, you want to protect it against disaster. This chapter deals with backing up and recovering a database, as well as some other unusual system problems you might encounter when working with a MySQL database.

Backing Up

It is vital to back up your data regularly. The actual backup strategy you use depends on many factors, including how often your database is updated and the severity of the consequences of your database being offline.

You should schedule your backups so that, should the worst happen, recovery onto a new database server can be done quickly and with no mission-critical data lost.

Taking a Full Backup

```
mysqldump --user=user --host=host --port=port \
          --password=password dbname > filename.sql
```

The mysqldump command outputs the contents of a database as a series of SQL files. Each table is converted into a CREATE TABLE statement, and the data rows are converted into an INSERT statement. The SQL commands are output to screen by default, so you should redirect the output of this command to a filename to create a backup file.

The name of the database to back up comes after the connection options. You can then optionally specify the names of tables to extract—if you do not supply any table names, the entire database is dumped. The following command would dump only the book and person tables from the sample database:

```
mysqldump --user=zak --password=phrasebook \
  sampdb book person > sampdb.sql
```

The host and port options were omitted in the previous example, so this command would try to connect to a MySQL server running on the default port on the local machine.

If you want to specify multiple databases for mysqldump, use the --databases switch. All subsequent words are treated as database names. The following command dumps the contents of two databases named db1 and db2:

```
mysqldump --user=zak --password=phrasebook \
  --databases db1 db2 > dump.sql
```

To dump all the databases on your MySQL server in one operation, use the --all-databases switch.

Taking an Incremental Backup

```
log-bin
```

A full database backup can be quite an intensive process. Every row from every table has to be returned to the mysqldump program, and then each line has to be written to a file. Running a full database backup on a busy server can affect performance for users.

The alternative is to use incremental backups that MySQL implements via its binary logging feature. To activate binary logging, add the log-bin option to my.cnf and restart the MySQL server. Alternatively, start mysqld with the --log-bin switch.

Binary logs are written to the home directory for the mysql user, usually /var/lib/mysql. The default filename is *hostname*-bin.*XXX*, where *hostname* is the server's hostname and *XXX* is a sequence number. Each time the MySQL server is restarted or you issue the FLUSH LOGS command, a new binary log is started.

The binary log contains any SQL statement issued that might have updated data. Any UPDATE, INSERT, or DELETE is recorded, even if no changes were made as a result of that command—for instance, an UPDATE statement where the WHERE clause matched no rows. This level of logging allows you to roll the database forward from a full backup right up to the very latest database change that was made.

In order to restore successfully, your binary logs must begin with transactions that took place immediately after a full backup was taken. To synchronize the binary log with a backup file, use the --flush-logs option to mysqldump, which causes a FLUSH LOGS command to be issued as soon as the dump begins. Any further database activity is then written to the next binary log in sequence.

As you might expect, writing the binary log does have an effect on your server's performance, but the benefits gained usually outweigh the performance lost. According to the MySQL documentation, MySQL runs approximately 1% slower with binary logging enabled—a very minor decrease.

Restoring from a Backup

Now that you have a comprehensive backup strategy, let's examine how you would go about restoring your database from the backup files should a catastrophe happen.

Restoring a Full Backup

```
mysql --user=user --host=host --port=port \
    --password=password dbname < filename.sql
```

As the output from mysqldump is simply a series of SQL commands, you can restore a database in a single operation by passing the contents of the backup file into the mysql program.

If you restore to the same *dbname* from which the dump was taken, the existing tables are overwritten. A DROP TABLE statement is included in the output from mysqldump for each table that was backed up.

If the backup file is for a single database, it does not contain a CREATE DATABASE statement, so you could actually restore the entire database file to a different database name by specifying a different database name in the mysql command.

If mysqldump was run with the --all-databases or --databases option, the CREATE DATABASE command is automatically included for each database in the backup.

Restoring an Incremental Backup

```
mysqlbinlog hostname-bin.XXX | mysql \
     --options dbname
```

Before restoring an incremental backup, you must restore your database to a known point using a full backup, and then use a binary log file—or series of files—that contains the database changes from that point onward.

The mysqlbinlog utility converts the binary log format to a text format containing the SQL commands that have been recorded. The output from mysqlbinlog can then be passed into a mysql command just like the output from mysqldump.

The preceding phrase uses a pipe to feed the output from mysqlbinlog into mysql, but you could also save the output to a file and then pass it to mysql using file redirection.

The following command uses a regular expression to restore a database using every binary log file in the current directory. The shell reads the list of matching files and passes each one to mysql.

```
mysqlbinlog hostname-bin.[0-9]* | \
    mysql --options dbname
```

Because the numbers in the filenames are padded with leading zeros, the shell reads the files in the correct sequence. If you restore manually from more than one binary log file, you must use the backup files in the correct order.

Corrupted Table Data

```
CHECK TABLE table;

REPAIR TABLE table;
```

Occasionally the MySQL data files might become corrupt and need repairing. The easiest way to check the integrity of a table is by using the CHECK TABLE SQL command. The following command checks the book table for errors:

```
CHECK TABLE book;
```

If the output looks similar to the following, the table is okay and does not need any further action:

```
+-------------+-------+----------+----------+
| Table       | Op    | Msg_type | Msg_text |
+-------------+-------+----------+----------+
| sampdb.book | check | status   | OK       |
+-------------+-------+----------+----------+
```

Sometimes, however, you see errors in the Msg_text column telling you about problems with the table. When this happens, issue the REPAIR TABLE command, and MySQL attempts to fix the problem.

The myisamchk utility that ships with MySQL can be used to check and repair MyISAM tables with a higher degree of flexibility than the SQL commands. When myisamchk is run with no options, it simply checks a table for errors. A number of command line switches can be added to gain additional information or instruct the utility to begin a repair process.

The MyISAM table files that myisamchk examines are stored in your data directory and have .MYI file extensions. If your data directory is /var/lib/mysql, you can check all the tables in the sampdb database using the following command:

```
myisamchk /var/lib/mysql/sampdb/*.MYI
```

The usual way to perform a quick table check is to use the --fast switch, which checks only tables that have not been properly closed.

The --medium-check option performs a more thorough check of the tables and finds the vast majority of errors. The --extend-check option is the most thorough option but is very slow—only use this if --medium-check does not find a problem.

After you have determined that a table file is corrupt, you can repair it using the --recover switch. Before repairing a table with myisamchk, you should stop mysqld—you do not want the MySQL server writing to your table files while you repair them.

Sometimes myisamchk reports that it cannot fix a problem using this option and then you should try using --safe-recover instead. This option is much slower but also more thorough.

Server Crash

If your MySQL server keeps crashing, it's time to file a bug report. Even though MySQL is thoroughly tested, there might still be rare bugs, and you should know how to begin to diagnose this kind of problem.

First, you should make sure that it is actually the MySQL server that is crashing and not your client program. Check the amount of time that the server has been up by issuing the `mysqladmin version` command. The output contains a line like this:

```
Uptime: 109 days 23 hours 31 min 51 sec
```

In this case, the server has been running for a long time, so it is clear that `mysqld` did not crash. Instead, you need to debug your client program.

If the uptime reported is very small or `mysqld` is not running at all after a suspected crash, the first step is to check that your tables are not corrupt. Stop `mysqld` and run the following command from the data directory to check every table in the system:

```
myisamchk --silent --force */*.MYI
```

Restart `mysqld` with the `--log` switch, or add `log` to the [mysqld] section of `my.cnf`. Every SQL command is logged to a file, and you should try to find a way to reproduce the crash consistently using the same command. You should then query the bugs database at http://bugs.mysql.com/ before filing a bug report.

Another possible cause of your crashes is an underlying hardware problem. In particular, faults with your system's RAM or hard drives can cause peculiar errors in MySQL. Perform a thorough check on your system's hardware if you experience intermittent, unexplained server crashes.

Common Errors

This section lists some of the most common error messages you will encounter and the steps necessary to work out what is wrong.

Can't Connect to MySQL Server

```
ERROR 2002: Can't connect to local MySQL server
through socket '/var/lib/mysql/mysql.sock' (2)

ERROR 2003 (HY000): Can't connect to MySQL server
on '123.45.67.89' (113)
```

Usually these errors mean that there is no mysqld process running on the server machine.

If you are unable to connect to a local MySQL server, check your system's process list using ps on Unix or Task Manager on Windows and start the MySQL server if it is not running.

It's possible that the local socket file has been removed. The default location is /tmp/mysql.sock, and some systems periodically clean out the contents to /tmp. It could even be that another user has deleted this file—inadvertently or otherwise—because the /tmp directory is often writable by all users. If you experience this issue, change the location of the socket file to another directory owned by the mysql user by adding these lines in my.cnf:

```
[mysqld]
socket=/path/to/mysql.sock

[client]
socket=/path/to/mysql.sock
```

To check that mysqld is listening on the port you are expecting, use the netstat command to check that it is indeed accepting network connections. On Unix/Linux use this command:

```
shell> netstat -1
```

On Windows, the command is slightly different:

```
> netstat -a | find "LISTENING"
```

If you are unable to connect to a remote MySQL server and you are sure mysqld is running, check your firewall settings. You must allow TCP/IP traffic on port 3306—or whatever other port the server runs on—to allow remote connections.

Note that this error message only indicates an incapability to communicate with a MySQL server, not an authentication problem. If you are able to connect to mysqld but use an invalid password, you see one of the errors from the next section.

Access Denied

```
ERROR 1045 (28000): Access denied for user
'user'@'host' (using password: YES)
```

You might have supplied an incorrect username or password, or a database name that the given username does not have access to when connecting from the current host. Check the privilege tables in the mysql database to make sure the connection arguments are correct.

If you use the short -p switch instead of --password, remember that the password must follow immediately with no space. Otherwise the argument following -p is treated as the database name.

Too Many Connections

```
ERROR 1040: Too many connections
```

The maximum number of simultaneous connections allowed is defined in the `max_connections` system variable, and the default value is 100. A new value can be set in `my.cnf` using the following lines:

```
[mysqld]
max_connections=200
```

Increasing the `max_connections` value is usually not the answer. MySQL has exceeded the maximum number of connections for a reason, and you should try to find out why it ran out. You should only increase this value if you are sure your system can support more connections.

In fact, `mysqld` allows one more connection than the specified number, so a superuser can connect even when the maximum connections have been exceeded. To diagnose problems, run the `mysqladmin processlist` command and try to work out why there are so many connections.

MySQL Server Has Gone Away

```
ERROR 2006: MySQL server has gone away
```

This error usually indicates a timeout where `mysqld` has closed the connection with the client. The default timeout interval is eight hours, but this value can be changed using the `wait_timeout` system variable—its value is in seconds. When this error is the result of a timeout, the `mysql` program attempts to reconnect automatically.

You also see this error if the `mysqld` process stops running while you are connected to a MySQL server—even if it is restarted instantly. If `mysql` is unable to reconnect, you should check whether `mysqld` is still running.

Got Error from Table Handler

```
Error 1030: Got error 141 from table handler
```

This error indicates an internal problem with the database table storage file. It can usually be fixed using the `myisamchk` utility. The error number reported in this message indicates the nature of the problem. Use the `perror` command from the shell to find the corresponding error message.

```
shell> perror 141
141 = Duplicate unique key or constraint on write
      or update
```

When you encounter this kind of error, you should stop `mysqld` and run `myisamchk --recover` on the corresponding `.MYI` file.

Sometimes the errors reported are symptomatic of other system issues, as in the following case:

```
$ perror 28
Error code  28:  No space left on device
```

Getting Help

If you have a troublesome problem and feel you need help to figure it out, you can look to several places. First of all, make sure you have read the relevant

sections of the online manual at http://
dev.mysql.com/doc/refman/5.0/en/index.html.

Several MySQL mailing lists cover a wide range of
topics, and lists are available for regional user groups
and different languages. Check http://lists.mysql.com/
for the latest mailing lists—there will almost certainly
be one where you can ask for assistance.

MySQL AB provides technical support for an annual
fee with various service levels for those who need the
assurance of having somewhere to turn when things
do go wrong. All support packages include access to
the MySQL Knowledge Base, a searchable library of
technical articles that often gives you the answers you
need very quickly.

The higher levels of support include 24-hour,
7-days-a-week telephone assistance, guaranteed
emergency response time, and remote troubleshooting
by a MySQL expert. For more information, see
www.mysql.com/support/.

TROUBLESHOOTING AND EMERGENCIES

Appendix A

A Brief MySQL Tutorial

In this appendix you're going to briefly walk through the entire process of creating and using a database, from designing tables and creating users to adding indexes and querying tables. The focus is on a mix of explaining and doing—the intent is to quickly get you productive with MySQL.

The database you'll build in this appendix will be used to store information about books and book loans from a tiny library. The database won't be too complex— you will just store the essential pieces of data such as

- The title, condition, and author of books in the library
- The names and email addresses of people who borrow books
- The details of when books were loaned to people

Getting Started

Before you can start running the examples in this chapter, you need to have

- Access to an installation of MySQL. We recommend installing a copy on your own computer for testing. Even though this sounds daunting, it isn't—MySQL installs easily on many platforms, including BSD, Linux, Mac OS X, Solaris, and Windows. For more information, refer to the online manual.

- An account on the MySQL server that has full permissions on one or more databases. The root account created by default in a fresh install of MySQL has all the required permissions.

- A MySQL client. We recommend using the mysql command-line client or the MySQL Query Browser. (All the examples in this chapter assume you're using the mysql command-line client.) See Chapter 7, "The mysql Command-line Client," for more details.

Creating a Database

A database is a container for data sets. These data sets are modeled by and stored in tables. Databases (along with tables) also provide objects that MySQL users can be granted access to, allowing the activities of a user to be mostly restricted to what is inside of one database or just a set of one or more tables.

In this chapter, you'll create a database called library. Before you do, you should check the other databases in this MySQL installation and ensure that the database does not already exist.

Showing Existing Databases

Because users are assigned rights to specific databases, the current user can only see the databases for which he has rights. If you're logged in as the MySQL root user, all databases should be visible.

To view a list of databases, run the following query:

```
SHOW DATABASES;
```

This should return a list of the existing databases. If querying a new MySQL installation, there will be two databases:

- The mysql database (which contains administrative data and documentation for the MySQL server)
- The test database (which is commonly used as a sandbox where ideas and features can be safely tested)

If the server is not a new installation, it will probably contain additional databases.

The output of the SHOW DATABASES command should look something like this:

```
+-----------------+
| Database        |
+-----------------+
| mysql           |
| test            |
+-----------------+
```

Running the CREATE DATABASE Command

If the MySQL server you are querying does not already contain a database called library, create the database as follows. (If a database called library exists, substitute a different name in the following command and in the subsequent examples.)

```
CREATE DATABASE library;
```

Your MySQL client should display a message like

```
Query OK, 1 row affected (0.01 sec)
```

If you run the SHOW DATABASES query again, you will see that the library database has been created.

Creating Tables

Now that you have a database, you can start to design tables that both model the library data and act as containers for it.

First, set the database within which you will create the tables using the USE command.

```
USE library;
```

Designing Tables

Designing tables is a difficult skill to teach. Although there are principles to guide the design of tables, the applicability of the principles can be limited by performance and storage requirements. This appendix cannot teach you everything, but it at least points you in the right direction for creating your own tables.

Jumping Right In

One of the easiest ways to learn about table design is to follow along with someone designing a set of tables. This appendix walks you through the steps of designing your table.

The first thing to do is think about what information you need to store. In the case of this little library, you need to store information about

- The books that you have (book title, author, and condition)

- The people who borrow books (name and email address)

- The book loans that you have made (which book was loaned to which person at what time)

You could store much more information in your tables, but this will do for illustrative purposes.

A naïve table design for this data is a table that contains a column for each piece of information: book title, book author, book condition, borrower name, borrower email, and so forth.

One major problem with this design is that there is a large amount of duplicated data. Every time you lend out *In the Night Kitchen*, for example, you would have to record all of the data on the book in the table. This ends up being tremendously inefficient, both in terms of storage and processing effort. In some cases, duplication is unavoidable (or even desirable), but in most cases the duplication is clearly a waste.

To address this redundancy, you will place the most commonly duplicated sets of data (books and borrowers) in their own tables. You will also put loans into their own table that includes columns that reference entries in the book and person tables.

Designing Your First Table

The first table is going to contain information about the title, author, and condition of each book. Each of these pieces of data will be stored in its own column, while each row will contain a full set of information about a book.

Choosing a Primary Key

Your first choice is to determine if you want to use one of your candidate keys for your primary key or if you want to create a synthetic primary key. A *candidate key* is a column or set of columns that can uniquely identify a row within a table. A *primary key* is a candidate key that has been chosen (or created) as the candidate key that best identifies a row.

You have four possible candidate keys:

- The book title
- The book title combined with the author's name
- The book title combined with the book's condition
- The book title combined with both the author's name and the book's condition

The last candidate key is the most accurate, but it still does not allow you to safely have multiple copies of a book, and it isn't even remotely usable, given its length.

If you use a synthetic value as a primary key, you can simply assign a number to each row. In the case of the book table, this requires much less storage space than using the candidate key. In addition, by using a synthetic primary key, you can modify all the data values in the row without worrying about other tables that might be using the primary key as a foreign key.

Defining Columns

Each column in the table has a name and is defined according to the type of data it contains and the maximum length (and, in some cases, the format) of the data it can store. You're going to use a synthetic value as the primary key in your book table, so this column for the primary key will be one of the integer data types.

Before you choose the exact column type, you need to know the rough range of numbers you want to store in the column. In the case of your library, you can arbitrarily decide that you won't have more than 50,000 books. This allows you to use an UNSIGNED SMALLINT column (which can store integers between 0 and 65,535) for storing your primary key.

The columns that store the book title and book author data will contain character data rather than numeric data. MySQL has three column data types for character data: CHAR and VARCHAR for storing strings between 0 and 255 characters, and various sizes of TEXT columns for storing what are usually larger amounts of data.

For both book title and book author, use a VARCHAR column and set the column width to 255 characters. That should give you enough space for almost any author or book name.

The drawback of this approach is that indexes for the VARCHAR column must be larger to accommodate the maximum possible width for a column. You can eliminate this penalty by forcing your indexes to only use part of the column. This is explained in the "Exploring Table Creation" section later in this chapter.

Finally, for the condition column, you need to decide how you want to denote the condition of a book. You could use an integer flag, where 0 stands for perfect condition, 1 stands for normal, and so on. You could go a step further and put the condition data into a separate table. Although this would reduce the amount of duplication, it seems excessive.

For cases like this, MySQL has a column type called ENUM. An ENUM-type column can contain any single value from a list of predefined values. The values stored in an ENUM column look like strings but are actually stored as numeric data. This strategy allows ENUMs to be very storage efficient. You will define an ENUM column to hold your condition data that can hold values of mint, fine, good, or poor.

Now that you've determined the data types required by each of your columns, you'll use SQL commands to create them.

Naming Columns

When naming columns, keep the following guidelines in mind:

- Always use lower case in identifiers.
- Name the table's primary key *table_id* and use the same name for foreign keys in other tables that reference this table's primary key. This allows you to easily search your SQL queries for all the references to a given table's primary key.

- Name the columns in a semantic manner. Give them titles that refer to their contents. Do not use SQL keywords such as date or index as titles.

- Use underscores to separate words in column names.

- Choose a convention for singular or plural names and then stick to it.

- Avoid using reserved words (such as condition) for column names.

So, with that information in mind, you'll create a table called book with the following columns:

- book_id
- title
- author
- cond

Creating the book Table

To create the book table, run the following command:

```
CREATE TABLE book (
  book_id SMALLINT UNSIGNED NOT NULL
➡ AUTO_INCREMENT,
  title   VARCHAR(255),
  author  VARCHAR(255),
  cond    ENUM('poor','good','fine','mint'),
          PRIMARY KEY (book_id)
);
```

Because this is a relatively complex query, it is discussed in detail in the "Exploring Table Creation" section later in this chapter. This gives you the chance to move on to more commonly used tasks more quickly.

Note that the exact amount of whitespace (tabs, new lines, or spaces) within most of a query is not semantically important—that is, it doesn't mean anything to the MySQL server. To the server, all that matters is that at least one character of whitespace is placed between separate words. Because of MySQL's flexibility in this regard, it is easy to construct SQL queries that are easy for both humans and MySQL to read. The exception to this behavior is within string literals. `'lib ary'`, for instance, is quite different from `'library'`.

Creating the person Table

In addition to your table for storing book information, you also need tables to store information on people who are borrowing books, as well as the book loans that are made.

For the `person` table, you need columns to store the person's name and email address. Once again, you need a primary key so you can refer to a given row in the table from another table. Again, use a synthetic primary key, as the available candidate key (a combination of the person's name and email address) is too long to be practical.

When choosing the field type for your primary key, you need to estimate the number of people who are likely to borrow books from your library. Again, you can arbitrarily define your values, saying that, at most, a few hundred people might borrow books. You can easily store this range within an `UNSIGNED TINYINT` column (which can store integers between 0 and 255).

The name and email columns are similar to the title and author columns in the book table. You can set them to `VARCHAR(255)`.

The query for creating the table could look like this:

```
CREATE TABLE person (
  person_id TINYINT UNSIGNED NOT NULL
➥ AUTO_INCREMENT,
  name      VARCHAR(255)
            COMMENT "The person's name",
  email     VARCHAR(255)
            COMMENT "The person's email address",
            PRIMARY KEY (person_id)
) COMMENT "Basic information about book borrowers";
```

Although this table is similar to the previous table, note that COMMENT keywords are used here to add explanatory information about the table and individual columns. Even though the comments don't add much value here, comments can provide valuable information to help people understand what a given table or column is for and why a table has been designed in a certain way.

Creating the loan Table

For the loan table you need to correlate a date to an entry in the book table and an entry in the person table. You will need columns for storing

- A primary key for the table (that, once again, will be synthetic)
- A primary key from the book table
- A primary key from the person table
- The date when you lent a book to someone

The resulting table creation statement could look something like this:

```
CREATE TABLE loan (
  loan_id   INT UNSIGNED NOT NULL AUTO_INCREMENT,
  person_id TINYINT UNSIGNED NOT NULL,
  book_id   SMALLINT UNSIGNED NOT NULL,
  date_lent DATE NOT NULL,
            PRIMARY KEY (loan_id)
) COMMENT "Store info on book loans";
```

You should be familiar with each of the column types used here, with the exception of DATE. DATE columns, as implied by the name, can store dates between '1000-01-01' to '9999-12-31' (in the Gregorian calendar). When inserting a date into a DATE column, you can use a YYYY-MM-DD or YYYYMMDD notation—for example, July 25, 2005 could be written as '2005-07-25' or 20050725.

Populating Tables with Data

Now that you've created your tables, the next step is to populate them with data. The sample data you are using is taken from the author's childhood memories (that, happily, extend from about 1973 to the present day).

Although there are a variety of ways to get data into MySQL tables, you'll use the SQL INSERT statement because it is the most common way to get data into a table. The INSERT statement creates a new row at the end of a table. The basic format of the command is

```
INSERT [INTO] [db_name.]table_name
(list, of, columns, ...)
VALUES (list, of, values, ...)
```

For example, to enter information on a slightly good copy of the Canadian classic, *Jacob Two-Two Meets the*

Hooded Fang by Mordecai Richler, you would use this
query:

```
INSERT book (author, title, cond)
VALUES ('Mordecai Richler',
        'Jacob Two-Two Meets the Hooded Fang',
        'good');
```

This INSERT query breaks down into these major parts:

- **INSERT**—The optional INTO modifier was omitted
  after the INSERT keyword in this case. In general,
  shorter commands are better, as long as the readability of the commands is not hindered. Although
  INSERT INTO is arguably clearer than INSERT, the
  INSERT command is so commonly used that it is
  fairly safe to assume that anyone reading the query
  will understand what you mean.

- **book**—The name of the table in which to insert
  data immediately follows the INSERT (or INTO) keyword. If no database name is specified, the table
  name is assumed to be a part of the default database (as set with the USE statement). If no default
  database has been specified, you would have to
  specify the name of the database before the name
  of the table—library.book, for example.

- **(author, title, cond)**—After the name of the
  table, the list of columns into which the data will
  be inserted is specified. The list is enclosed in
  parentheses, and each column in the list is separated by commas. If a column is omitted from the
  list, the field will be populated by the default
  value for the column.

  The list of columns is optional. Rather than
  explicitly specifying the column names, you could

specify values for each column in the order the column occurs within the table. This is a dangerous shortcut because it is easy to insert data into the wrong columns.

Note that the book_id column was not specified in this list; this is intentional. The book_id column is an auto-increment column. When a new row is inserted into the table, as long as the INSERT statement that generates the row does not include the auto-increment column, a value will be automatically inserted into the column. The value generated is equal to the largest existing value in the auto-increment column plus one.

- **VALUES (...)**—One or more sets of data to be inserted into the table can follow the VALUES clause. Each set of data must correspond to the columns defined earlier in the query. Each value in the list is separated by a comma. Text values are enclosed in quotes; numeric values are not.

If you're inserting multiple rows of data, place a comma after the closing parenthesis of each row (if it is the final row, use a semicolon). For example, to insert three more rows of data into the book table, run this command:

```
INSERT book (author, title, cond)
VALUES ('Maurice Sendak',
        'In the Night Kitchen',
        'mint'),
       ('Caroll Spinney',
        'How to Be a Grouch',
        'poor'),
       ('Dr. Seuss', 'Green Eggs and Ham', 'good');
```

In addition to reducing the amount of typing that needs to be done, inserting multiple rows of data with a single SQL query has the advantage of efficiency: MySQL has to do less work than if it had to process three separate queries.

Now that you have entered books to loan, you can start loaning the books to people. Say that Carl wants to borrow *In the Night Kitchen*. First, you enter him into the person table using the following statement:

```
INSERT person (name, email)
    VALUES ('Carl', 'carl@example.com');
```

Then you need to create an entry in the loan table. To do this, you must know the primary keys for Carl and for the book he wants to borrow.

First, look up the primary key for Carl

```
SELECT person_id FROM person WHERE name = 'Carl';
```

You should get a result something like

```
+-----------+
| person_id |
+-----------+
|         1 |
+-----------+
1 row in set (0.07 sec)
```

NOTE

Because we know there are only a few records in the sample database and there is only one Carl, this query is fine for finding the primary key value. Of course, with larger databases you might have to perform a query using several fields to be sure that you have identified the correct record.

Next, you need to find the primary key for *In the Night Kitchen*:

```
SELECT book_id FROM book
WHERE title = 'In the Night Kitchen';
```

You should get back a value of 2.

Now you can create an entry in the loan table using the two primary keys that you retrieved and a MySQL function:

```
INSERT loan (book_id, person_id, date_lent)
VALUES (2, 1, '2005-07-25');
```

You'll have to use some of these primary keys several times. Rather than try to remember them, you can store them in user variables. A *user variable* is simply a name (in a special format) that correlates to a piece of data. The basic form of the user variable is @*name*. The name portion of a user variable can contain a to z (upper or lowercase), 0 to 9, $, ., and _. A variable can be used in any context where a numeric or string value would normally be used.

To assign a value to a user variable, use the := operator. For example:

```
SELECT @fish := 'Herring';
```

Running another SELECT on the user variable simply returns the value assigned:

```
SELECT @fish;
```

Knowing about user variables, you can rewrite your queries to be easy to run and less error prone:

```
SELECT @person_id := person_id FROM person
      WHERE name = 'Carl';
SELECT @book_id := book_id FROM book
      WHERE title = 'In the Night Kitchen';
```

```
SELECT @date := '2005-07-25';
INSERT loan (book_id, person_id, date_lent)
VALUES (@book_id, @person_id, @date);
```

Notice how the variable names are used instead of the literal values. This allows you to use the same INSERT query over and over to populate the loan table. All you need to do is change the WHERE clauses as you add new loans.

You can further optimize this by combining all of your queries that retrieve data into one query:

```
SELECT @book_id := book_id,
       @person_id := person_id,
       @date := '2005-07-25'
  FROM book, person
 WHERE book.title = 'In the Night Kitchen'
   AND person.name = 'Carl';
```

This type of SELECT is called a *join*. Joins allow a single SELECT statement to retrieve data from two or more tables. In this query, you simply combine your three separate queries into one query that joins two tables. More on joins (and subqueries) is found in Chapter 4, "Retrieving Data: Simple Queries."

Notice that the table name is included with the columns—in this case, book.title. Although MySQL is often able to sort out which columns go with which tables in many cases, a change to a table involved in this query could break the query if you aren't explicit.

Now you just run your INSERT query the same as last time:

```
INSERT loan (book_id, person_id, date_lent)
VALUES (@book_id, @person_id, @date);
```

For one final optimization, you can make another change to the query—you can combine all of the separate queries into a single query that combines an INSERT and a SELECT statement. The syntax is quite simple. Replace the VALUES clause of an INSERT query with a SELECT statement that returns the right number of columns of data, as seen in the following code:

```
INSERT loan (book_id, person_id, date_lent)
SELECT book_id, person_id, '2005-07-25'
  FROM book, person
 WHERE book.title = 'In the Night Kitchen'
   AND person.name = 'Carl';
```

This allows you to eliminate the user variables and intermediate queries.

Why weren't you shown this query to begin with? Well, for novice DBMS users, the preceding query can be a lot to take in at one time. Understanding what separate queries compose the larger query makes it much easier to understand the larger query. If this query was too much for you, just remember a few things for the future:

- Most complex queries can become a set of small and simple queries.
- There is more than one way to do things.

Each of these techniques is useful on its own. If you are a novice user, start with small queries and build up from there. A broken simple query is much easier to fix than a broken complex query.

Exploring Table Creation

Now that you have created your tables and started working with them, the details of the CREATE TABLE statement are discussed next.

When you created your first table (book), you used this command:

```
CREATE TABLE book (
  book_id   SMALLINT UNSIGNED NOT NULL
➡ AUTO_INCREMENT,
  title     VARCHAR(255),
  author    VARCHAR(255),
  cond      ENUM('poor','fine','good','mint'),
            PRIMARY KEY (book_id)
);
```

Note the following characteristics of the CREATE TABLE command:

- **CREATE TABLE**—The CREATE TABLE command is used to create tables. In this case, a table named book will be created in the current database (as was selected via the USE statement).

- **Column definition**—Within the book table, you want to create four columns. The portion of the SQL statement that defines the columns (and indexes) is enclosed in parentheses. Each statement that defines a column or an index is separated by a comma.

  For each column, the name of the column is followed by the column's data type and any modifiers (such as UNSIGNED or NOT NULL). For example, title VARCHAR(255) defines a column called title that can contain from 0 to 255 characters.

- **Index definition**—Indexes are defined using the INDEX or KEY clause. Index definitions are slightly different than column definitions. The general form is

```
INDEX optional_name (list, of, columns, ...)
```

The INDEX statement (the KEY statement can also be used) asserts that you want to define an index. After this, you can give the index a name (if desired). In general, this is not needed. After the optional name is a required list of one or more columns enclosed in parentheses. Additionally, each column in the column list can be only partially indexed—that is, instead of indexing the full width of the entire column, a smaller portion can be indexed. The benefit of this approach is that the index can be updated more rapidly and less space is required for the index. The drawback is that the index is less accurate. However, in most cases, this is not a problem. The syntax for this is

```
INDEX optional_name (column(length), ...)
```

To index only the first 20 characters of the title of a book, you would add this index definition statement to your table definition: INDEX (title(20)).

- **Primary key definition**—In MySQL, primary keys are a special form of index that is defined using the PRIMARY KEY clause. The syntax for the primary key definition is much the same as the definition for an index. The major difference is that no optional name can be used for a primary key.

Adding Indexes to Existing Tables

You don't have to add indexes at the same time that you create a table. You can add indexes to existing tables using the CREATE INDEX command. The exact syntax is very similar to the INDEX clause of a CREATE TABLE command:

```
CREATE INDEX index_name
ON table_name(list, of, columns, ...)
```

For example, in the book table, you might want to speed up ordering and matching operations on the title column. Adding an index to the title column is a good way to do this. To add the index, run the following query:

```
CREATE INDEX title ON book (title(16));
```

The index is explicitly limited to the first 16 characters of the title. This gives you an accurate index but is much more efficient for storage than placing an index of up to 255 characters.

Finding Information About Tables

You aren't always dealing with databases and tables that you have created. Here are some handy commands for helping you explore tables.

To list all of the tables in the default database, run

```
SHOW TABLES;
```

The command should output something like the following:

```
+-------------------+
| Tables_in_library |
+-------------------+
| book              |
| person            |
| loan              |
+-------------------+
3 rows in set (0.00 sec)
```

To view tables in a database other than the default database, use a FROM clause with the name of the database from which you want to view the tables. For example, to show a list of all tables in the test database, run this command:

```
SHOW TABLES FROM test;
```

To view the definition of a table, several tools are at your disposal. To only view information on the columns in the table, use the DESCRIBE command. Syntax for the command is

```
DESCRIBE [database_name.]table_name;
```

To show information on the columns in table book, run

```
DESCRIBE book;
```

The output of the command is quite wide. Run the command yourself and then follow along as the DESCRIBE command is discussed.

The information that DESCRIBE generates has the following meaning:

- **Field**—The name of the column being described. Arguably, this should be called column rather than field.

- **Type**—A description of the type and maximum width of the column. The format is the name of the type, followed by the width enclosed in parentheses. Column types and, in part, widths have already been discussed. Note here that some columns for which you did not define a width are shown as having widths. Each column type has a default width and a maximum width. If a column is defined without a width, the default width is assigned. For integer-type columns, the width is the maximum width of the largest number that can be stored in the column. In general, you only need to define explicit widths for CHAR or VARCHAR columns and FLOAT- or DECIMAL-type columns.

- **Null**—NULL is a value that represents nothing. NULL values are often used to represent cases such as a column never having been filled in or an unknown quality. The author avoids using them, as they require a set of special operators to deal with and test them. By default, columns in MySQL allow NULL values. In the future, in most cases, you will define columns explicitly as NOT NULL—doing so saves a little bit of storage and gives you simpler tables with which to work.

- **Key**—Key contains information about the indexes on the column. Primary keys are marked PRI. Other values are MUL, indicating that the column is part of an index that allows duplicate values in the column; and UNI, that indicates that the column is part of an index that only allows unique values.

Note that a column that is part of a unique index might still be flagged as MUL if the column can contain NULL values or is part of a multicolumn UNIQUE index.

- **Default**—Each column in MySQL has a default value associated with it. Default values are used in cases where an INSERT statement does not specify a value for a column. If you were to insert data into the book table, for example, using this query:

```
INSERT book (title) VALUES ('Inferno');
```

the columns not explicitly mentioned in the query (book_id, author, and cond) would have the default value for the column inserted. Try it and see what the result looks like; run the preceding command and then run

```
SELECT * FROM book WHERE author IS NULL;
```

The output should resemble:

```
+---------+---------+--------+-----------+
| book_id | title   | author | condition |
+---------+---------+--------+-----------+
|       5 | Inferno | NULL   | NULL      |
+---------+---------+--------+-----------+
1 row in set (0.00 sec)
```

Since you don't need this information, you should get rid of it:

```
DELETE FROM book WHERE author IS NULL;
```

- **Extra**—Contains extra information on a column, such as if it auto-increments or is unique.

Creating Users

A *user* is a name associated with a set of authentication credentials with an associated set of permissions. During the installation of MySQL, a user (called root) is created who has full rights to all the databases within that instance of MySQL. This user's power is similar to that of the root user on Linux and should only be used when necessary.

At a minimum, each database stored within a single instance of MySQL should probably have its own administrative user account. If the database will be used by multiple users, each class of user should have its own account.

Creating a User

In this section, the mysql command-line client is used to create a user with full rights to the library database. (See Chapter 7 for instructions on loading the command-line client.)

```
GRANT ALL ON library.* TO librarian@localhost
    IDENTIFIED BY 'secret';
```

This command is parsed as follows:

- **GRANT ALL**—The GRANT keyword is immediately followed by a list of privileges to grant. Alternately, use the ALL keyword to grant all privileges (except the GRANT privilege that allows a user to grant rights to other users) to the user.

- **ON library.***—The ON clause is used to specify on which database(s) and tables within the database(s) privileges will be granted. In the example, you are granting all privileges (except GRANT) on all tables (noted by the asterisk *) in the library database.

- **TO librarian@localhost**—The TO clause allows you to specify an account name at a given host to which to grant permissions.
- **IDENTIFIED BY 'secret'**—The IDENTIFIED BY clause allows you to set a password for the account—in this case, 'secret'.

To view the new user, run the following command:

```
SHOW GRANTS FOR librarian@localhost;
```

For more information on permissions and users, see Chapter 6, "User Management and Security."

Summary

This appendix provided a quick tutorial on some of MySQL's basic features but skipped many key materials. To handle tasks that weren't covered here, review the index and Chapter 1, "Maps of MySQL," to find the right section of the book to help you.

Index

INDEX

How can we make this index more useful? Email us at indexes@samspublishing.com

163

How can we make this index more useful? Email us at indexes@samspublishing.com

165

INDEX

How can we make this index more useful? Email us at indexes@samspublishing.com

169

INDEX

How can we make this index more useful? Email us at indexes@sampspublishing.com

171

N

How can we make this index more useful? Email us at indexes@samspublishing.com

173

INDEX

How can we make this index more useful? Email us at indexes@samspublishing.com

175

INDEX

INDEX

How can we make this index more useful? Email us at indexes@samspublishing.com

179

INDEX

How can we make this index more useful? Email us at indexes@samspublishing.com

181